UNDERSTANDING RHETORIC

2nd Edition

a GRAPHIC GUIDE to WRITING

Elizabeth Losh
Jonathan Alexander
Kevin Cannon
Zander Cannon

bedford/st.martin's
Macmillan Learning

BOSTON • NEW YORK

For Bedford/St. Martin's

Vice President, Editorial, Macmillan Learning Humanities: Edwin Hill
Editorial Director, English: Karen S. Henry
Senior Program Director: Leasa Burton
Program Manager: Molly Parke
Executive Editor: Carolyn Lengel
Senior Production Editor: Ryan Sullivan
Media Producer: Melissa Skepko-Masi
Senior Production Supervisor: Jennifer Wetzel
Executive Marketing Manager: Joy Fisher Williams
Indexer: Schroeder Indexing Services
Senior Photo Editor: Martha Friedman
Permissions Manager: Kalina K. Ingham
Senior Art Director: Anna Palchik
Cover Illustrators: Kevin Cannon, Zander Cannon
Printing and Binding: LSC Communications

Manufactured in the United States of America.

2 1 0 9 8 7
f e d c b a

For information, write: Bedford/St. Martin's, 75 Arlington Street, Boston, MA 02116
(617-399-4000)

ISBN 978-1-319-04213-4

Acknowledgments

CONTENTS

PREFACE: GETTING GRAPHIC

When we first began to work on *Understanding Rhetoric*, we expected other composition instructors to respond well to this comic-style text. We saw that comics were being assigned more frequently in writing courses, and we hoped our book would encourage students to engage deeply with core concepts of writing and rhetoric. By emphasizing multimodal approaches to composing, we wanted to engage student writers in thinking about their identities, contexts for their research, and effective writing processes. We also wanted to create a book that students would actually *want* to read—a book that could make rhetoric interesting and maybe even enjoyable.

> I REALLY LIKE THIS BOOK -- IT FILLED A NICHE FOR OUR STUDENT POPULATION THAT WAS OVERDUE TO BE FILLED.
>
> Sonja L. Andrus,
> *University of Cincinnati*

But we were still surprised by the level of enthusiasm that greeted *Understanding Rhetoric*, which shook up writing classrooms at more than 450 colleges and universities and which, instructors told us, got "nothing but positive responses from students." We were, and are, delighted that so many have responded so positively to the book. And we've benefited enormously from feedback from instructors and students who have been using it in their classrooms.

And so *Understanding Rhetoric*, Second Edition, was born. You'll find that this book still covers all the commonly taught topics in first-year composition, offering time-tested techniques for improving critical analysis, argumentation, and the development of research questions in college writing. As in the first edition, it contains practical tips for improving organization, identifying bias, evaluating sources, representing scholarly debates, and avoiding plagiarism. It includes new attention to collaborative writing, including peer review, and many new examples that students can use as models for analysis of their own. As always, it incorporates the latest research in composition, which focuses on the development of writers as well as writing.

> I LIKE THE FACT THAT IT'S ACCESSIBLE, BUT MORE THAN ANYTHING IT IS RHETORICALLY AWARE.
>
> Chris Gerben,
> *St. Edward's University*

Increasingly, composition instructors recognize that students need a range of literacy skills. The Web, video, blogging, YouTube, Tumblr, and social networking sites complement and challenge traditional text-based literacy practices, and students must consider the rhetorical requirements of writing for multimodal platforms—and must also see graphic design and visual evidence as basic tools for communication. After all, many of them may be doing most of their writing using such platforms. The graphic approach of *Understanding Rhetoric* supports instructors who want to teach with a book that—like the works their students interact with regularly—is both visually and textually rich.

> UNDERSTANDING RHETORIC PRACTICES WHAT WE PREACH ABOUT MULTIMODAL RHETORIC.
>
> Sarah F. McGinley,
> *Wright State University*

Understanding Rhetoric is arranged like a comic anthology, with nine issues dealing with individual rhetorical concepts. Each issue gives an in-depth look at the topic, reviews important points, suggests ways for students to put the concepts to use in their own work, and offers assignment ideas.

- Every issue begins with a chapter that takes a narrative approach to the rhetorical concept being discussed. The author characters interact with historical and fictional characters in comic panels that reward careful reading and that make complex ideas engaging and memorable.

- A "ReFrame" section after the chapter features student characters, Luis, Cindy, and Carol, grappling with the concepts and "walking through" a variety of texts.

- A "Drawing Conclusions" spread at the end of each issue suggests assignments that will allow students to try the concepts out for themselves.

Building on feedback from classroom users of *Understanding Rhetoric*, the second edition includes additional support for helping students get more out of peer review, for managing identities in context, and for doing research with library databases. It also includes more examples and quick advice for putting concepts into action. Look for the following new material:

- A new "Walk the Talk" feature in each chapter that walks students through analyzing an example text and reflecting on how they can use the chapter's concepts in their own reading, writing, and research

- Up-to-date advice on self-presentation in Chapter 3, "Writing Identities"

- A new Chapter 5, "Composing Together," which addresses the benefits of working together and practical strategies for making collaborations—including peer review—work smoothly

- An updated "ReFrame" section for Chapter 6, "Wrong Turns or Shortcuts?," featuring an expanded discussion of database research

In addition, the detailed instructor's manual will help both novice and experienced instructors plan a course around *Understanding Rhetoric*.

As you read through the text with your classes, ask students to pay attention not only to what the characters are saying, but to *how* information about writing and composing is conveyed both textually and visually. Our hands-on style emphasizes an active approach to writing, reading, and responding to all kinds of texts and emphasizes the dialogic nature of successful academic and public writing.

THIS IS THE MOST SUCCESSFUL TEXT I HAVE EVER TAUGHT WITH IN TERMS OF STUDENT ENTHUSIASM.

Jim Haendiges,
Dixie State University

Ultimately, to enter into conversations (in good Burkean fashion) in different public spheres, writers should work through a series of interactions and discussions that allow them to craft insightful positions and compelling arguments. Our characters show how all writing is connected to identities. People write from particular positions, stances, and senses of self, and having a greater awareness of those positions—social, cultural, political, and historical—makes for more sophisticated and assured composing.

We hope you and your students enjoy *Understanding Rhetoric*. Most importantly, feel free as you teach with this book to talk back to us. Dare to disagree, either with us or other characters in the book. Get graphic with the text, and invite your students to draw and write within it. You might find yourself working with your students to make your own graphic guide to writing!

AUTHOR ACKNOWLEDGMENTS

We appreciate the contributions of the many, many individuals whose expertise and advice made this book possible.

Reviewers
We received invaluable feedback from a wonderful group of reviewers, whose suggestions helped us shape the direction of individual chapters and of the book as a whole during its entire development process:

Susan Achziger, Community College of Aurora; John Alberti, Northern Kentucky University; Ira Allen, American University of Beirut; Sonja Andrus, University of Cincinnati, Blue Ash College; Matt Barton, St. Cloud State University; David Beach, West Virginia University; Christiane Boehr, University of Cincinnati; Jeanne Bohannon, Kennesaw State University; Malkiel Choseed, Onondaga Community College; Jennifer deWinter, Worcester Polytechnic Institute; Summer Dickinson, Mid-Plains Community College; Misty Evans, Murray State University; Diana Fernandez, Barry University; Chris Gerben, St. Edward's University; Jim Haendiges, Dixie State University; Sabrina Hardy, Liberty University; Wendy Hayden, Hunter College of the City University of New York; Chris Cormier Hayes, Simmons College; Marcy Isabella, Stockton University; William Lalicker, West Chester University; Bonnie Markowski, University of Scranton; Christine Masters, Purdue University; Jessica Matthews, George Mason University; Sarah McGinley, Wright State University; Erin McLaughlin, University of Notre Dame; Jessica Miller, Eastern Michigan University; Elizabeth Monske, Northern Michigan University; Jill Morris, Frostburg State University; Alice Myatt, University of Mississippi; Jessica Nastal-Dema, Georgia Southern University; Danielle Nielsen, Murray State University; Kate Pantelides, Eastern Michigan University;

Michael Pemberton, Georgia Southern University; Melody Pugh, United States Air Force Academy; Rachael Ryerson, Ohio University; Molly Scanlon, Nova Southeastern University; Marc Scott, Shawnee State University; Kassia Shaw, Waubonsee Community College; Aleksandra Swatek, Purdue University; Benjamin Syn, University of Colorado, Colorado Springs; Heidi Thoenen, University of Akron; Stephanie Vie, University of Central Florida; Shevaun Watson, University of Wisconsin–Eau Claire; Kristen Weinzapfel, North Central Texas College; Chantay White-Williams, Southwestern Illinois College; Jennifer Williams, Chandler-Gilbert Community College; Julie Winslett, University of North Georgia; and Melody Wise, Glenville State College.

Contributors
We would like to acknowledge some of the people whose ideas and suggestions helped in the creation of this book: Norah Ashe, University of Southern California; Greg Benford, University of California, Irvine; Vinayak Chaturvedi, University of California, Irvine; Michael Clark, University of California, Irvine; James Paul Gee, Arizona State University; Brook Haley, University of California, Irvine; Michael Householder, Southern Methodist University; Julia Lupton, University of California, Irvine; Steven Mailloux, Loyola Marymount University; Lynn Malley, University of California, Irvine; Michele Mason, University of Maryland; Robert Moeller, University of California, Irvine; Erika Nanes, University of Southern California; Miriam Posner, University of California, Los Angeles; Terri Senft, New York University; Ellen Strenski; Brook Thomas, University of California, Irvine; Phil Troutman, George Washington University; and Ann Van Sant, University of California, Irvine.

Many thanks to Marissa Osato, a graduate of the University of California, Irvine, for allowing us to adapt content from her essay on Japanese Americans in internment camps during World War II; Uzair

Mohammad, a graduate of the University of California, San Diego, for allowing us to adapt content from his LinkedIn page; and Mel Chua for making her graphic research paper "What Is Engineering?" available with a Creative Commons license.

We are very grateful to Tom Gammill for his illustrations in Chapter 6.

Special thanks are in order to Keith McCleary and Jasmine Lee for their work on the instructor's manual, which was radically redeveloped for this edition.

For contributions to our initial thinking on instructional materials for *Understanding Rhetoric*, our gratitude goes to Henry Jenkins, Emily Roxworthy, Molly Scanlon, Cynthia Selfe, and Wayne Yang.

We are grateful to Thomas LeBien of Hill & Wang and to Jessica Marshall for helpful initial feedback on this project.

Finally, we would like to thank Zander Cannon and Kevin Cannon, our coauthors, for turning our manuscript into a real comic book. They contributed not just illustrations, but also many great ideas for conveying concepts visually—and a lot of good jokes.

Bedford/St. Martin's

Everyone on the team at Bedford/St. Martin's was critical for bringing this second edition to fruition. Constructive and creative feedback—from Leasa Burton, Carolyn Lengel, Molly Parke, and others—over the course of many lively conversations was central to our writing process. We are grateful to Anna Palchik for her art direction; to our project editor, Ryan Sullivan; and to our marketing manager, Joy Fisher Williams.

Elizabeth Losh, *The College of William and Mary*
Jonathan Alexander, *University of California, Irvine*

We would like to thank everyone at Bedford/St. Martin's for their support, encouragement, and enthusiasm over the course of making this book. In particular we'd like to thank Leasa Burton, Carolyn Lengel, and Molly Parke for their vision and guidance in seeing this book through from an idea to a finished project, and we'd like to thank Anna Palchik, Deb Baker, and Ryan Sullivan for their support on the art and technical end.

Big thanks also go out to our coauthors, Liz and Jonathan, for being nimble with their script and adaptable to the peculiarities of making a comic book, and to all the additional challenges of making that comic book informative and educational. Finally, we appreciate the support of Thomas LeBien, who recommended us as artists for *Understanding Rhetoric* in the first place.

Also, Zander would like to thank his wife, Julie, and their son, Jin, for their support and for making their home a happy place to return to at the end of the day.

Kevin Cannon
Zander Cannon

SPACES FOR WRITING

In this issue...

DISCOVERING CONTEXTS FOR WRITING

THIS BOOK -- IN ITS CONTENT, ITS FORMAT, AND ITS LAYOUT -- PLAYS WITH THE IDEA THAT PEOPLE WRITE IN MANY DIFFERENT PLACES AND SPACES.

New Release!

SELF-HELP REFERENCE ??

UNDERSTANDING RHETORIC
2nd Edition
a GRAPHIC GUIDE to WRITING
LOSH · ALEXANDER · CANNON · CANNON

NOT NECESSARILY IN THIS KIND OF SPACE --

-- THOUGH HUMANS HAVE SENT MESSAGES TO THE STARS --

-- BUT IN DIFFERENT SOCIAL SPACES THAT AFFECT HOW WE COMMUNICATE, WHAT IS SAID, WHAT IS NOT SAID...

...AND HOW OUR MESSAGES ARE RECEIVED, UNDERSTOOD, AND ACTED UPON.

LIZ

JONATHAN

OFTEN, WHEN PEOPLE TALK ABOUT BEGINNING A WRITING PROJECT, THIS IS WHAT THEY THINK ABOUT:

THE BLANK PAGE.

IT'S A WAY TO VISUALIZE ISOLATION, SOLITUDE, AND LONELINESS; STRUGGLING WITH ONE'S SOUL IN A PRIVATE ROOM; AGONIZING OVER WORD AFTER WORD; DILIGENTLY WAITING FOR **INSPIRATION**!

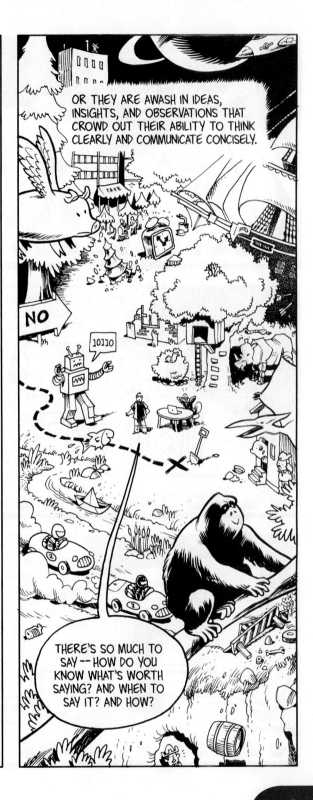

OR THEY ARE AWASH IN IDEAS, INSIGHTS, AND OBSERVATIONS THAT CROWD OUT THEIR ABILITY TO THINK CLEARLY AND COMMUNICATE CONCISELY.

THERE'S SO MUCH TO SAY -- HOW DO YOU KNOW WHAT'S WORTH SAYING? AND WHEN TO SAY IT? AND HOW?

Introduction

GOING BOLDLY THROUGH WRITING PROCESSES

HEY, IT'S ZANDER CANNON, ONE OF THE ILLUSTRATORS OF THIS BOOK.

WHAT'S UP, ZANDER? TAKING A BREAK?

WHAT? OH, HI, GUYS.

ACTUALLY, I'M WORKING.

I NEED TO GET A PROJECT UNDERWAY, AND SOMETIMES THE BEST WAY FOR ME TO START IS JUST TO LET MY THOUGHTS WANDER.

REALLY? I DO THAT, TOO!

I OFTEN LET MY THOUGHTS WANDER ALL OVER THE PAGE -- WHETHER IT'S A PAPER PAGE OR A DIGITAL "PAGE."

SOMETIMES I EVEN SEND TEXT MESSAGES TO MYSELF ABOUT THINGS THAT INTEREST ME, OR ABOUT A PROJECT I'M WORKING ON.

...AND THAT MAY BE ONE OF THE MOST IMPORTANT LESSONS ABOUT LEARNING TO WRITE AND COMMUNICATE EFFECTIVELY.

WHEN WE WERE WORKING ON THIS COMIC, FOR INSTANCE, WE KNEW THAT WE WOULD HAVE TO REVISE WHAT WE WROTE BASED ON WHAT THE ILLUSTRATORS DREW.

SOMETIMES KEVIN AND ZANDER DREW EXACTLY WHAT WE HAD IN MIND.

AND OTHER TIMES, THEY HAD **BETTER** IDEAS.

FAINT!

RHETORIC

UNCORRECTED PROOF

IF WE HADN'T ALL BEEN WILLING TO WORK WITH OTHERS' SUGGESTIONS, WE WOULD HAVE HAD A VERY LIMITED AND UNSATISFACTORY BOOK!

"Perfect manuscript"

SO WORKING COLLABORATIVELY FROM THE BEGINNING WAS A CRUCIAL COMPONENT OF OUR COMPOSING PROCESS.

AND NOW, BECAUSE WE ARE USING BOTH IMAGES AND WORDS TO CONVEY OUR ADVICE, WE WANT TO SAY SOMETHING ABOUT VISUAL LITERACY.

EXPLORING VISUAL LITERACY

(Photos) Mack McCoy

CONSIDER THIS: WHEN A PHOTOGRAPH APPEARS IN THE PAGES OF A GRAPHIC NOVEL, WE KNOW THAT IT HAS A SPECIAL SIGNIFICANCE.

IT LOOKS DIFFERENT FROM THE OTHER PICTURES ON THE PAGE.

IT SEEMS TO DEPICT MORE ACCURATELY THE WAY THAT SOMEONE OR SOMETHING LOOKS IN REAL LIFE.

SO, AT THIS MOMENT, A PERSON WHO OPENS TO THESE PAGES IN THIS BOOK CAN COMPARE THE APPEARANCE OF THE CARTOON ME TO THE ME OF THE PHOTOGRAPH.

IT DOESN'T TAKE CAREFUL VIEWING TO SEE THAT THE ARTISTS HAVE SIMPLIFIED AND ABSTRACTED THE WAY JONATHAN LOOKS.

IN COMPARISON, THE PHOTOGRAPH PROBABLY SEEMS MUCH CLOSER TO SHOWING THE "REAL TRUTH."

WE USUALLY ASSOCIATE HAND-DRAWN IMAGES WITH WORKS OF THE IMAGINATION...

...WHILE PHOTOGRAPHS CREATED BY A MACHINE LIKE A CAMERA ARE SUPPOSED TO GIVE US THE REAL STORY, THE FACTS.

HOWEVER, WE KNOW THAT, JUST LIKE A DRAWING, A PHOTOGRAPH IS REALLY ONLY A REPRESENTATION.

AFTER ALL, I CAN'T REACH IN AND ACTUALLY TOUCH THIS DESK.

MAYBE I CAN.

BUT THE READER CAN'T. IT'S A STATIC IMAGE THAT EXISTS ONLY IN TWO DIMENSIONS ON THE PAGE.

A PHOTOGRAPH IS NOT JUST A "PICTURE OF REALITY."

THERE ARE ACTUALLY MANY CONCEPTUAL DIMENSIONS TO ANY IMAGE.

THIS SECTION OF OUR BOOK IS ABOUT WHAT IMAGES MEAN AS WELL AS SHOW.

I WONDER WHAT THOSE STUDENTS ARE LAUGHING ABOUT?

JUST ADDING WORDS CAN CHANGE THE ENTIRE MEANING OF AN IMAGE.

AND THE FRAMING OF THE CONTENT MATTERS, TOO.

FOR EXAMPLE, WHEN AN IMAGE IS CROPPED IN A CERTAIN WAY, OR WHEN AN ILLUSTRATION SHOWS A DETAIL INSTEAD OF ZOOMING OUT TO SHOW A BIGGER PICTURE, THE ENTIRE MEANING OF THE IMAGE CAN CHANGE.

IN THIS VERSION, WE DON'T SEE A PROFESSIONAL SETTING.

THE IMAGE SENDS A VERY DIFFERENT MESSAGE WITHOUT THE OFFICIAL AND IMPOSING BACK-DROP OF AN OFFICE.

THEN, IF WE SEE MORE INFORMATION IN THE FRAME, THE MEANING CHANGES YET AGAIN.

THIS VERSION OF THE IMAGE IS MUCH MORE PLAYFUL AND SUBVERSIVE.

(Photos) Mack McCoy

15

A SINGLE PHOTOGRAPH MAY BE SELECTED FROM A SERIES OF SIMILAR IMAGES BECAUSE IT "READS WELL" OR "TELLS A CLEAR STORY."

LEARNING TO READ THE DIFFERENT ELEMENTS OF A VISUAL TEXT IS PART OF WHAT WE CALL VISUAL LITERACY.

VISUAL LITERACY IS VERY IMPORTANT IN UNDERSTANDING THE MESSAGES THAT ARE CONVEYED BY PHOTOGRAPHY AND ILLUSTRATION...

...AND BY PAINTING, GRAPHIC DESIGN, SCULPTURE, ARCHITECTURE, VIDEO -- ANY MEDIA THAT WE ENGAGE WITH OUR EYES.

WHEN WE SEE IMAGES IN A WORK OF ART OR IN A FILM, WE PAY ATTENTION TO THE CRAFT OF INTENTIONAL COMPOSITION.

WE MAY NEED TO LOOK VERY CLOSELY AND INVEST TIME TO UNDERSTAND HOW THE VISUAL ELEMENTS TELL A STORY.

OUR CULTURE HAS TAUGHT US THAT DEPICTING CLOSENESS OR DISTANCE IN AN IMAGE MIGHT SUGGEST SOMETHING ABOUT THE INTIMACY BETWEEN THE PEOPLE SHOWN.

BECAUSE VISUAL LITERACY

IS SUCH AN IMPORTANT PART

OF OUR **CULTURE**,

WE HAVE CHOSEN TO

CREATE THIS BOOK

IN THE

FORM! OF! A! COMIC!

PART OF OUR DECISION TO WRITE A GRAPHIC BOOK HAS TO DO WITH THE PORTABILITY OF OUR **MESSAGE**.

INCREASINGLY, A VARIETY OF ARGUMENTS ARE BEING MADE AND SHARED THROUGH VISUALLY RICH MEDIA SUCH AS THE WEB.

...BUT MORE ON THAT IN LATER CHAPTERS.

17

THIS IS THE LOGO FOR THE HUMAN RIGHTS CAMPAIGN, A GROUP THAT WORKS FOR EQUALITY FOR LGBTQ AMERICANS.

THE CLEAN LINES OF THE IMAGE CERTAINLY GET YOUR ATTENTION.

THE GEOMETRY IS VERY SIMPLE, AND THE USE OF THE PRIMARY COLORS BLUE AND YELLOW MAKES THE HRC'S LOGO REALLY STAND OUT.

IT USES **NEGATIVE SPACE** TO DRAW THE VIEWER'S EYES TO THE CHANNEL BETWEEN THE TWO RECTANGLES, WHICH CONNECTS THE SPACES ON EITHER SIDE.

THE IMAGE ALSO USES **SYMMETRY**.

TOP AND BOTTOM AND RIGHT AND LEFT MIRROR EACH OTHER.

IF WE READ THE IMAGE CAREFULLY, WE SEE THAT THE HUMAN RIGHTS CAMPAIGN LOGO GETS OUR ATTENTION, BUT IT ISN'T INTENDED TO SHOCK US.

IT IS AN IMAGE OF HARMONY AND BALANCE.

CRITICS MIGHT EVEN SAY THAT IT IS AN IMAGE ABOUT NOT STANDING UP OR STICKING OUT.

(Photo) Mack McCoy

REFRAME with **Luis & Cindy**

Why rhetoric? Why a **COMIC BOOK?**

Odio cuando mi madre insiste en hablar en vietnamita frente a la gente.

[I HATE IT WHEN MY MOTHER INSISTS ON SPEAKING IN VIETNAMESE IN FRONT OF PEOPLE.]

MY DAUGHTER IS VERY GOOD WITH LANGUAGES.

I CAN SEE THAT.

Yo no estaba coqueteando contigo. Yo sólo estaba siendo amable.

[I WASN'T FLIRTING WITH YOU. I WAS JUST BEING FRIENDLY.]

WHOOPS!

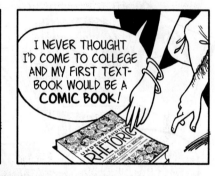

I NEVER THOUGHT I'D COME TO COLLEGE AND MY FIRST TEXT-BOOK WOULD BE A **COMIC BOOK!**

I KNOW WHAT YOU MEAN.

I **LIKE** COMICS, BUT I DON'T THINK OF THEM AS **TEXTBOOKS.**

C'MON, IT'S ONLY THE FIRST DAY OF CLASS.

KEEP AN **OPEN MIND!**

MY MOM'S READING IT TOO!

SHE'S TAKING NIGHT CLASSES, AND HER TEACHER IS USING THE SAME BOOK!

I NEVER THOUGHT I'D BE GOING BACK TO SCHOOL SO LATE, BUT AT LEAST MY DAUGHTER AND I CAN STUDY TOGETHER!

BUT MY CLASS IS ACTUALLY **HARDER** THAN HERS.

WE'RE ALSO **CREATING** GRAPHIC NOVELS THAT TELL THE STORIES OF OUR OWN LIVES.

THEY'RE CALLED **MEMOIRS**, MOTHER.

GRAPHIC MEMOIRS.

MY SPANISH MAY NOT BE GREAT, BUT MY ENGLISH IS FINE.

I HOPE YOU DON'T TALK THIS WAY TO **YOUR** MOTHER.

PART OF WRITING A **GRAPHIC MEMOIR** IS HAVING TO DRAW **ONESELF!**

I'M A LITTLE **INTIMIDATED.**

IN MY WRITING CLASS, SOME OF THE STUDENTS ARE REALLY GREAT AT DRAWING!

BUT THERE ARE A LOT OF THINGS THAT THOSE STUDENTS **DON'T** KNOW HOW TO DO.

LIKE **PAY ATTENTION.**

SOME OF THEM HAVE MANNERS THAT ARE ALMOST AS BAD AS HERS.

COME ON, MOM. I'M SURE THAT THE OTHER STUDENTS AREN'T REALLY THAT BAD.

YOU SHOULD TRY TO MAKE FRIENDS.

I DON'T WANT TO TALK ABOUT OUR PERSONAL BUSINESS.

YOU SHOULDN'T BE EMBARRASSED, MOM.

AND BEING A GOOD ARTIST DOESN'T REALLY MATTER AS MUCH AS YOU THINK IT DOES.

IT SOUNDS LIKE THE PROJECT IS ABOUT TELLING A COMPELLING STORY AND MAKING AN INTERESTING VISUAL ARGUMENT.

LIKE IN MY LAB REPORT HERE, I HAVE TO USE THESE CHARTS AND GRAPHS TO CONVINCE THE TEACHER THAT I'VE DONE THE EXPERIMENT CORRECTLY.

CHARTS AND GRAPHS ARE ONE THING. BUT WHAT DO I DO WITH THIS PAGE SHOWING MY TIME IN THE REFUGEE CAMP ENGLISH CLASS?

...IT FEELS TOO **DENSE** OR SOMETHING.

ACTUALLY, IT'S REALLY INTERESTING TO SEE HOW MUCH INFORMATION YOU PACK INTO THE PAGE.

BUT WHAT IF YOU REALLY DEVELOPED THE CHARACTER OF YOUR TEACHER?

YOU COULD BREAK UP THIS FRAME INTO INDIVIDUAL FRAMES, AND WE WOULD KNOW THAT YOU WERE SHOWING DIFFERENT EPISODES IN TIME.

COMING UP IN THE NEXT EXCITING EPISODE OF **REFRAME**

"What does ARISTOTLE have to do with ME?"

[pg. 57]

DRAWING CONCLUSIONS

The following assignments ask you to try out the
concepts discussed in this Introduction.

1 Start a journal in which you make a list
of the genres and visual metaphors you
see throughout *Understanding Rhetoric*
(like the science-fiction elements in the
Introduction). After each chapter, write
a response discussing how visual elements
affect your interpretation of the book.

Keep the journal all semester, and at the end
of the course write a final reflection about
how your discussion of visuals changed from
the beginning to the end of the course.

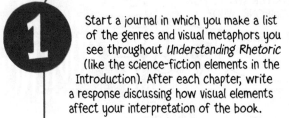

2 Try to read just the text—
not the images—on page 2
of the Introduction.

Write or talk with your
classmates about what you think
this text means. Then examine
the illustrations on page 2.

What do the visuals seem to
say on their own? How do they
change the meaning of the text?

3

In the ReFrame for this chapter, Carol is working on her graphic memoir. Using both words and images, make a draft of what your own graphic memoir might look like.

What would you choose to emphasize? How would you make your central ideas and themes clear?

4

Comic artists often arrange panels to suggest different perceptions of time. Browse graphic novels or other comics to find creative depictions of the experience of passing time. Then create a storyboard for a short comic about an event that seemed to you to occur much more slowly or more quickly than you know it actually did.

Present your storyboard to others in your class and get feedback on how well your method works.

IS THAT A RHETORICAL QUESTION?!!

HMF.

SOME PEOPLE CALL A QUESTION **"RHETORICAL"** BECAUSE NO ANSWER IS ACTUALLY EXPECTED.

DO I LOOK **STUPID** TO YOU?

ACCORDING TO THEM, RHETORIC AND RHETORICAL ARE ALL ABOUT **SHUTTING DOWN** CONVERSATION AND DEBATE!

BUT I--

ACTUALLY, THE ANCIENTS DEVELOPED THE CONCEPT OF **RHETORIC** TO **FACILITATE** DISCUSSION.

THEY THOUGHT THAT RHETORIC PROVIDED A SET OF SKILLS THAT HELPED PEOPLE FOREGROUND IDEAS --

-- DISCUSS AND DEBATE THEIR THOUGHTS WITH OTHERS --

-- AND POTENTIALLY REACH COMMON GOALS OR MAKE DIFFICULT DECISIONS.

IN THE ORIGINAL GREEK, THE WORD **RHETORIC** COMES FROM THE VERB **EIRO**, "TO SAY."

memories feelings logic

BUT RHETORIC IS MUCH MORE THAN JUST **TALK**.

IT'S A WAY OF **THINKING** ABOUT HOW WE TALK...

values

insights

...THAT TAKES INTO CONSIDERATION THE ENTIRE SITUATION IN WHICH THAT TALK TAKES PLACE.

beliefs

RHETORIC IS ABOUT THE **SPACES** IN WHICH WE WRITE, CONVERSE, DEBATE, AND SHARE **IDEAS**.

REANIMATING ANCIENT VIEWS OF RHETORIC

MANY COMMONLY HELD NEGATIVE IDEAS ABOUT RHETORIC CAN BE TRACED TO THE ANCIENT GREEK PHILOSOPHER **PLATO**.

HE BELIEVED THAT TEACHERS LIKE US WHO TAUGHT RHETORIC WERE INSTRUCTING THEIR STUDENTS TO DECEIVE OTHERS RATHER THAN TO BETTER THEMSELVES.

IF SERIOUS DISCUSSION IS LIKE GYMNASTICS, THEN RHETORIC IS LIKE **COSMETICS**.

RHETORIC IS INTENDED ONLY TO HIDE FLAWS, NOT ENCOURAGE SELF-IMPROVEMENT.

PLATO (427–347 BCE)
ANCIENT GREEK PHILOSOPHER, STUDENT OF SOCRATES, AND FOUNDER OF THE ATHENIAN ACADEMY, AN IMPORTANT EARLY SCHOOL OF THOUGHT.

AS FAR AS PLATO WAS CONCERNED, RHETORIC WAS AN EMPTY, UNWHOLESOME DISTRACTION THAT TOOK ATTENTION AWAY FROM IMPORTANT PHILOSOPHICAL AND CIVIC MATTERS.

INDULGING THE POPULATION'S APPETITE FOR RHETORIC IS AS BAD AS SELLING **PASTRIES** INSTEAD OF DISPENSING **MEDICINE**.

PLATO ALSO THOUGHT THAT VIVID MEDIA EXPERIENCES, SUCH AS ANCIENT GREEK TRAGEDIES THAT SHOWED EXPLICIT SEX AND VIOLENCE, WOULD HAVE A BAD INFLUENCE ON YOUNG PEOPLE.

ALL POETS AND PLAYWRIGHTS SHOULD BE **BANISHED**!

41

PLATO FELT THAT THE YOUNG SHOULD BE PROTECTED FROM AMBIGUOUS MORAL MESSAGES.

PRETENDING TO BE CRIMINALS CAUSES CHILDREN TO GROW UP TO BE CRIMINALS IN REAL LIFE. EVERYONE KNOWS THAT.

PLATO WASN'T JUST WORRIED ABOUT CHILDREN. HE BELIEVED THAT THE INVENTION OF WRITING IN THE ANCIENT WORLD ALLOWED ADULTS TO LIE ABOUT THE TRUTH, PRETEND TO BE SOMEONE THEY WERE NOT, OR FORGET THE PAST AND TRADITION.

JUST AS PEOPLE WORRY TODAY ABOUT MANY OF THE EFFECTS OF TECHNOLOGY ON WRITING, PLATO WORRIED ABOUT THE EFFECT OF WRITING ON OUR ABILITY TO SPEAK THE TRUTH.

eHarmonium

Please Describe Yourself:
(Be ACCURATE!)
NAME:
STUDICUS MAXIMUS
HAIR:
FLOWING
HYGIENE:
IMPECCABLE
DENTAL ISSUES:
NONE
DURATION:
MODEL

THINGS WERE SURE A LOT BETTER BEFORE WE HAD WRITING!

PLATO'S STUDENT **ARISTOTLE** HAD A VERY DIFFERENT VIEW ABOUT WRITING AND RHETORIC.

PLATO   ARISTOTLE

ARISTOTLE WAS A PROPONENT OF THE USE OF RHETORIC TO PUT ACROSS A BROAD RANGE OF IDEAS.

ARISTOTLE (384–322 BCE)

ANCIENT GREEK PHILOSOPHER (AND STUDENT OF PLATO) WHOSE THINKING CONTRIBUTED MUCH TO THE DEVELOPMENT OF WESTERN EMPIRICAL AND SCIENTIFIC THOUGHT.

ARISTOTLE THOUGHT THAT PLAYS COULD SERVE AN **EDUCATIONAL** PURPOSE BY ENCOURAGING GREEK CITIZENS TO DEVELOP THEIR CAPACITIES FOR PITY AND FEAR.

BY SEEING THE CONSEQUENCES OF SEXUAL AND VIOLENT CRIMES THAT WERE COMMITTED BY ACTORS ON STAGE, SPECTATORS COULD LEARN **NOT** TO IMITATE **BAD ACTIONS.**

IN **THE ART OF RHETORIC,**

ETHOS

IS THE CREDIBILITY THAT A SPEAKER OR WRITER BRINGS TO THE SUBJECT THAT HE OR SHE IS COMMUNICATING ABOUT.

> You should buy the newest model.

> You should keep the car you have.

> You should read medical journals to find out about treatments.

> You shouldn't read medical journals; they'll just confuse you.

WE TRUST CERTAIN KINDS OF PEOPLE MORE THAN OTHERS -- BECAUSE THEY HAVE EXPERTISE, OR BECAUSE THEY ARE WELL INFORMED ABOUT THE SUBJECT AT HAND.

PATHOS

IS THE USE OF EMOTION IN DEBATE OR ARGUMENT.

APPEALS TO PATHOS SURROUND US, PARTICULARLY IN VISUAL ARGUMENTS SUCH AS ADVERTISEMENTS AND MANY ONLINE VIDEOS.

LOGOS

IS THE APPEAL TO REASON, TO THE FORCEFULNESS OF A WELL-THOUGHT-OUT AND WELL-STRUCTURED POSITION.

> ALL HUMANS ARE MORTAL.

> PLATO IS HUMAN.

> PLATO IS MORTAL.

SOME ARGUMENTS MAKE MORE **LOGICAL** SENSE THAN OTHERS, AND MANY CONSIDER LOGOS TO BE CRITICAL IN THE DEVELOPMENT AND DISSEMINATION OF IDEAS AND VALUES.

LEARNING TO RECOGNIZE THESE CONCEPTS WILL HELP YOU UNDERSTAND OTHER PEOPLE'S ARGUMENTS.

YOU'LL ALSO STRENGTHEN YOUR OWN POSITION AND THE WAY OTHERS SEE YOU.

ETHOS PATHOS LOGOS

ETHOS PATHOS LOGOS

FOR EXAMPLE, AN ONLINE PROFILE IS A RHETORICAL SPACE IN WHICH ETHOS, PATHOS, AND LOGOS ARE VERY IMPORTANT.

ONLINE PROFILES ALLOW USERS TO CREATE RICH, ENGAGING, AND SOMETIMES SATIRIC SELF-PORTRAITS.

ocial Network

Jonathan is thinking about getting a new computer.

Plato: Pff! It would just be the shadow of the CONCEPT of a computer, anyway.

Aristotle: Ooh, but the new X432g's are so AWESOME! 1 DISLIKE

Jonathan wonders if he should eat some breakfast.

Aristotle: 1) Consider the pros and cons, 2) ask an expert, and 3) do it if you're hungry.

Jonathan likes:

Douglass Aristotle Jet-Skis

Lincoln Funny Hats The US Constitution

Asian Food Monkeys

THE MIX OF PICTURES, VIDEO, AND TEXT CAN ESTABLISH -- OR **DESTROY** -- YOUR CREDIBILITY, OR **ETHOS**.

FOR INSTANCE, IF JONATHAN, AS A PROFESSOR OF ENGLISH, HAS A PROFILE RIDDLED WITH TYPOS AND IMAGES OF HIM GETTING DRUNK WITH HIS STUDENTS...

Social Network

Jonathan: Oh HAI I am Drunk with studentz !!!1!!

HIS CRED-IBILITY MIGHT **RISE** WITH SOME, BUT FALL WITH MOST OTHERS.

IMAGES AND WORDS CAN ALSO CONTRIBUTE TO THE PATHOS OF A PAGE...

ONE DAY:

Liz: is fine, keeping busy with work.

BUT THE NEXT:

Liz: is mourning the loss of a beloved cat.

"SNOOKUMS"
1999   2012

CERTAINLY, **PATHOS** IS BEING USED HERE TO PROMOTE SYMPATHY FOR LIZ...

...AND PERHAPS GENERATE A FEW KIND WORDS FOR HER **PAGE**.

WE GENERALLY DON'T THINK OF SOCIAL NETWORK PROFILES AS MAKING "LOGICAL ARGUMENTS," BUT IN A WAY, THEY **ARE** MAKING ARGUMENTS--

-- ARGUMENTS ABOUT WHO WE ARE, WHAT WE ARE INTERESTED IN, AND WHY SOMEONE MIGHT WANT TO "FRIEND" US.

@JONATHAN: Are you trying to seem cool by having a social network homepage?

BUT RHETORIC ISN'T JUST ABOUT **SPACE**. IT IS ALSO ABOUT **TIME**.

BENDING TIME through KAIROS

ALL OF US HAVE HAD EXPERIENCES THAT WERE EMBARRASSING, INSULTING, HUMILIATING, OR DEMORALIZING.

OFTEN WE WISH THAT WE COULD HAVE TRAVELED BACK IN TIME TO SAY JUST THE RIGHT THING AT THAT PARTICULAR MOMENT.

WE MAY COME UP WITH THE PERFECT THING TO HAVE SAID MUCH LATER, BUT IT IS ALREADY TOO LATE.

TONGUE TIED

LUMP IN THROAT

SHORT OF BREATH

RACING HEART

BUTTERFLIES IN STOMACH

RUBBER KNEES

today: AUDITIONS 5-9 pm

I-I KNOW YOU ARE, BUT WHAT AM I...?

DEBATES ABOUT DIFFICULT ISSUES ARE OFTEN TIME-SENSITIVE.

...VOTING TO REDUCE SPENDING ON UNIVERSITIES...

REELECT ME

BUT...

TUITION BILL

OFTEN, THERE IS A NARROW WINDOW WITHIN WHICH ONE CAN SPEAK OUT TO AFFECT AN ISSUE.

NO TUITION HIKES

FUND HIGHER EDUCATION

NO MORE TUITION HIKES

IN A LEGAL PROCEEDING, PARTICIPANTS ARE EXPECTED TO SPEAK ONLY AT CERTAIN TIMES.

...right to peaceably assemble...

...AND PRAISE OR BLAME FOR PEOPLE IN THE PUBLIC EYE MAY SWAY OPINIONS AT CRUCIAL MOMENTS.

MY CONGRESSMAN STANDS UP FOR STUDENTS. DOES YOURS?

49

Panel 1:

KAIROS WORKS IN MANY WAYS, ESPECIALLY TODAY.

DIGITAL WRITERS WHO COMMUNICATE USING THEIR COMPUTERS OR MOBILE PHONES OFTEN FEEL COMPELLED TO HIT "SEND" OR "ENTER" AS RAPIDLY AS POSSIBLE TO KEEP UP WITH A FAST-MOVING ONLINE CONVERSATION.

EMAIL

to: PREZ   subj: LISTEN, YO

WARNING!
MESSAGE CONTAINS FORCEFUL LANGUAGE

I NEED TO SEND THIS EMAIL RIGHT AWAY TO THE PRESIDENT OF THE UNIVERSITY.

Panel 2:

BUT IT'S USUALLY BETTER FIRST TO CONSIDER BOTH THE APPROPRIATENESS OF YOUR MESSAGE **AND** THE TIMING OF YOUR REPLY.

DING!

EMAIL

to: PREZ   subj: LISTEN, YOU

SEND ANYWAY

&%$#@!

I HIT "SEND" BEFORE I MEANT TO!

Panel 3:

WRITERS OFTEN MISS THE LONG-TERM **APPROPRIATENESS** OF KAIROS WHEN THEY FOCUS ON THE IN-THE-MOMENT **RESPONSIVENESS** OF KAIROS.

IF YOU THINK ABOUT A RHETORICAL OCCASION **ONLY** IN TERMS OF REACTING QUICKLY, YOU COULD EASILY END UP WITH AN EMBARRASSING DISASTER.

EMAIL

to: PREZ   subj: LISTEN, YOU

YOUR MESSAGE HAS BEEN IRRETRIEVABLY SENT.

TENURE

Liz's Boyfriend is on the prowl.

Ladies like thi[s]

Plato: I [...] my bro, w[...] [...]nd time f[...]t?

Aristotle: [...] want to [...] tonig[...]

Liz's Boyfriend
Relationship Status:
FINALLY SINGLE!

FOR EXAMPLE, USERS OF SOCIAL NETWORK SITES OFTEN ANNOUNCE CHANGES IN RELATIONSHIP STATUS...

...OFTEN BEFORE THEIR **PARTNERS** ARE INFORMED.

ON THE OTHER HAND, WAITING TOO **LONG** CAN DOOM YOUR COMMUNICATION EFFORTS.

HAPPY V-DAY! :)

KISS ME I'M IRISH

MARCH

SOMETIMES, HOWEVER, PEOPLE MANAGE TO SAY THE RIGHT THING AT JUST THE RIGHT MOMENT, AND THOSE PARTICULARLY **APT** WORDS ARE REMEMBERED FOR **CENTURIES**.

FAMOUS LAST WORDS -- SUCH AS NATHAN HALE'S

"I only regret that I have but one life to lose for my country."

-- ARE STILL QUOTED TODAY.

THE ROMAN RHETORICIAN **MARCUS TULLIUS CICERO** REALLY UNDERSTOOD THE IMPORTANCE OF KAIROS.

FOR EXAMPLE, WHEN HE WAS ABOUT TO BE EXECUTED ON ARBITRARY POLITICAL GROUNDS HE SAW A MOMENT FOR GRACIOUS WIT:

"There is nothing proper about what you are doing, soldier...

"...but at least make sure you cut off my head properly."

CICERO (106–43 BCE)
ANCIENT ROMAN PHILOSOPHER, LAWYER, AND STATESMAN

AFTER ALL, ARISTOTLE WASN'T THE **ONLY** FAMOUS RHETORICIAN IN THE ANCIENT WORLD.

CICERO, WHO LIKE MANY CULTURED ROMANS **ADMIRED** THE ANCIENT GREEKS, TRAINED ORATORS FOR THE ROMAN **SENATE**.

"No one can speak well, unless he thoroughly understands his subject."

CICERO THOUGHT ABOUT THE "TEXTS" OF RHETORIC VERY BROADLY AND REALIZED THAT SPEECHES AND WRITING ARE NOT THE ONLY WAYS PEOPLE COMMUNICATE.

THE ROMANS DEVELOPED AN ELABORATE SYSTEM OF LAWS AND PUBLIC ENGINEERING PROJECTS TO REGULATE AN INCREASINGLY COMPLEX SOCIETY.

THESE **RES PUBLICA**, OR "PUBLIC THINGS," ARE WORTH CONSIDERING AS RHETORICAL ACTS AND SPACES.

AS ARCHEOLOGISTS KNOW, EVEN GOVERNMENT BUILDINGS AND TRIUMPHAL ARCHES CONVEYED MESSAGES TO CITIZENS IN THE ANCIENT ROMAN WORLD AND PRESENTED IMPLICIT ARGUMENTS ABOUT AUTHORITY, PARTICIPATION, AND SHARED VALUES.

THE ROMANS UNDERSTOOD THAT ARCHITECTURAL SPACES COULD BE RHETORICALLY IMPORTANT IN ESTABLISHING THE CULTURE ASSOCIATED WITH THE ROMAN WAY OF LIFE, MUCH AS ADVERTISERS TODAY TALK ABOUT "BRANDING" PRODUCTS.

WE STILL NEED SPACES TO DEBATE IMPORTANT ISSUES IN PUBLIC.

AND KNOWING SPECIAL LANGUAGE FROM THE FIELD OF RHETORIC CAN BE HELPFUL TO IDENTIFY EFFECTIVE -- AND INEFFECTIVE -- TECHNIQUES.

GREEK TERMS LIKE *ETHOS, LOGOS, PATHOS,* AND *KAIROS* MIGHT NOT BE WORDS THAT YOU ADD TO YOUR EVERYDAY VOCABULARY.

BUT YOU USE THE GENERAL CONCEPTS ALL THE TIME...

...IN PERSON AND ONLINE.

and Jonathan

Aristotle: haha nice hairstyle LOL

Plato: If you saw where the rain came from, you could never go back to your happy ignorance !!!!

Cicero: As the mature

REFRAME
with
Luis & Cindy

What does ARISTOTLE have to do with ME?

LUIS! — **WHAT'S UP?**

NOT MUCH. HEY, HERE'S A QUESTION. I HAVE TO BE OUT OF TOWN FOR MY BIG BROTHER'S GOING-AWAY PARTY, SO I WROTE AN EMAIL TO MY WRITING TEACHER SAYING I'D MISS CLASS.

WHAT DO YOU THINK?

TO: l.losh@univ.edu
SUBJECT: HEY

Hey Mrs. Losh: I'm super busy on Friday. Please let me know if we do anything important. TTYL.

Luis

UH, WELL... — **...MAYBE YOU'D BETTER START FROM SCRATCH.**

WHAT? WHAT'S WRONG?

WELL, I DUNNO. I THINK THAT IF I WAS YOUR TEACHER, I MIGHT BE KIND OF INSULTED.

INSULTED? I'M LETTING HER KNOW AHEAD OF TIME THAT I'M NOT GOING TO BE IN CLASS!

WELL, THAT'S TRUE. BUT YOU AREN'T TELLING HER WHY YOU HAVE TO BE GONE... AND YOU'RE ACTUALLY IMPLYING THAT HER CLASS TIME MIGHT NOT BE IMPORTANT!

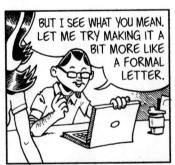

TO: l.losh@univ.edu
SUBJECT: Upcoming Absence

Dear Dr. Losh,

My older brother is on active duty in the military and is being deployed this month. My extended family will have his going-away party on Friday. I'd very much like to be there, given the circumstances. May I be excused from class? I'll be happy to make up any work, and I will ask my classmates for notes.

Sincerely,

Luis

TO: luis@univ.edu
SUBJECT: RE: Upcoming Absence

Dear Luis,

Thanks for the heads-up. We'll be starting brainstorming and process work on your first assignment, an analysis of the design of a print advertisement for an on-campus organization, service, or cause.

You should analyze the rhetorical strategies of the advertisement by commenting on its logos, pathos, ethos, and kairos. You should study details in the wording, images, typography, organization, and visual design on the page. Let me know if you have any questions, and I'll see you in class on Monday.

Best,
Liz

SILENT HIGH FIVE!

COOL. THAT'S VERY NICE OF HER.

AND NICE TO KNOW WHAT'S UP WITH THE FIRST WRITING ASSIGNMENT.

WHAT **AD** ARE YOU GOING TO CHOOSE?

I THINK I'LL DO THIS FLYER FOR **GAMMA GAMMA GAMMA!**

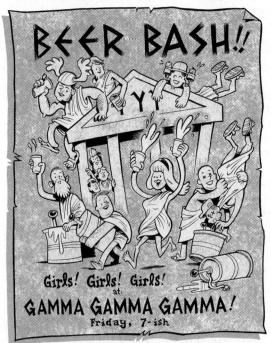

BEER BASH!!

Girls! Girls! Girls! at
GAMMA GAMMA GAMMA!
Friday, 7-ish

THERE'S A **KIND** OF PATHOS AT WORK HERE...

...BUT NOT A LOT OF **LOGOS!**

I SEE THAT. CHECK OUT THIS ONE FOR **BETA BETA BETA,** A SORORITY ON CAMPUS...

Calling all PROSPECTIVE PLEDGES!

JOIN US AT AN **INFORMATIONAL LUNCHEON** TO

★ Get a **HEAD START** on building your **RÉSUMÉ**!

★ Learn new **SKILLS**!

★ **NETWORK** with potential **COLLEAGUES** and **EMPLOYERS**!

SPONSORED BY

BETA BETA BETA

Monday, November 2nd
11 am – 1 pm

[*No Shorts or Jeans, Please!*]

SO WHICH MALE STUDENTS DOES **THAT** FLYER ADDRESS?

AND WHICH FEMALE STUDENTS ARE THE TARGET AUDIENCE **HERE**?

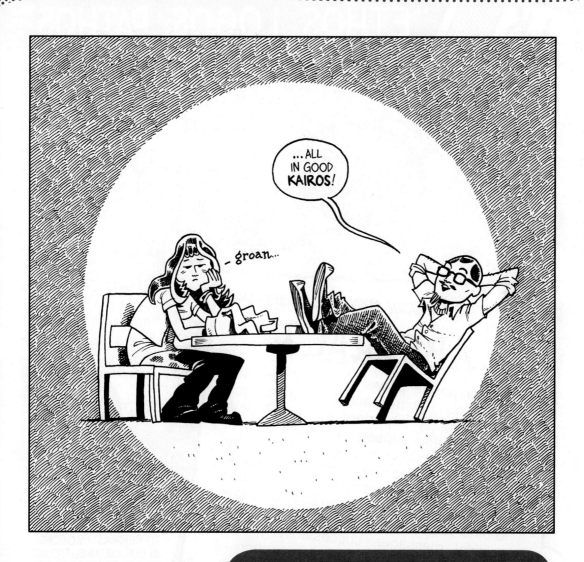

COMING UP IN THE NEXT EXCITING EPISODE OF **REFRAME**

"How do I **READ** this?"

[pg. 107]

DRAWING CONCLUSIONS

The following assignments ask you to practice thinking about the
rhetorical strategies of **ETHOS**, **LOGOS**, **PATHOS**, and **KAIROS**.

1 Keep your eye out for published texts
around campus: newspapers, flyers, posters,
zines, etc. When you find an interesting one,
grab a copy or take a picture of it.

Who is producing the text, and for whom?
What does the text aim to do, how does it
do it, and how effectively does it do it? Why
might this text exist on your college campus?
(Luis and Cindy perform a similar analysis in
the Reframe; how does the text you've
found compare to the ones they've found?)

2 Jot down some ideas about the rhetorical
characteristics of informal and formal
writing. In what ways are they similar?
In what key ways are they different?

Then, pick a kind of formal writing that
you either are working on now or have
encountered in the past.

Think about how a consideration of logos,
ethos, pathos, and kairos could help you
compose a formal piece better.

3

The Internet brings together diverse groups of people and invites them to share their ideas and opinions, so conflicts, disagreements, and arguments are common online.

Find a contentious or polemical exchange on one of your favorite Internet haunts. Dissect the appeals used by the various parties in the exchange. Look specifically for places where people lean on their reputation or expertise (ethos), where the participants solicit specific emotional responses from one another or from their audiences (pathos), and where logic, facts, or evidence are used (logos). What are the effects of using the appeals? Whose arguments are most convincing in this exchange, and why?

4

Your classmate has just heard that your instructor plans to test students on this chapter by requiring in-class essays summarizing the content, closed book.

In whatever text you see fit -- an email, a text message, an open letter, a social media rant, a formal letter to your instructor or someone else -- try to stop this in-class essay from happening!

Consider the rhetorical occasion and the context, and compose -- alone or with your classmates -- an effective rhetorical response. What appeals will be most effective for your audience? What genre feels most kairotic?

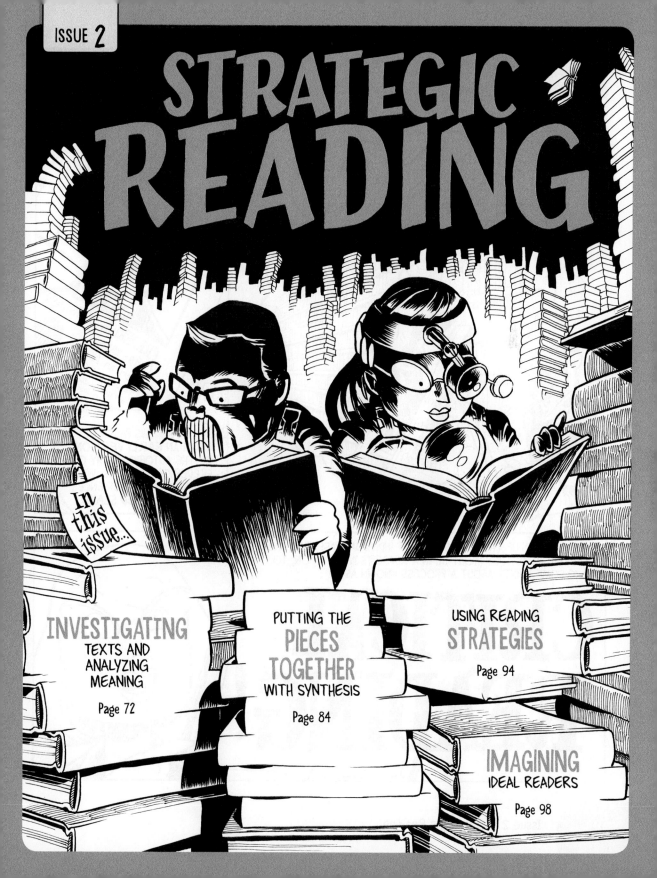

INVESTIGATING TEXTS AND ANALYZING MEANING

WHEN WE READ WE OFTEN SEE PICTURES IN OUR **MINDS**.

FOR EXAMPLE...

FREDERICK DOUGLASS (1818-1895) American Abolitioni... Orator, and Editor

...TAKE THIS PASSAGE FROM AN **EARLY VERSION** OF THE AUTOBIOGRAPHY OF FREDERICK DOUGLASS, WHO DESCRIBES HIS EXPERIENCES AS AN **ESCAPED SLAVE.**

WE'VE BROKEN UP THE WORDS SO THAT INDIVIDUAL PASSAGES ARE ILLUSTRATED, AS THEY MIGHT BE IN A READER'S IMAGINATION, TO MAKE SOME POINTS ABOUT A PROCESS KNOWN AS

CRITICAL READING!

"I have been frequently asked how I felt when I found myself in a free State. I have never been able to answer the question with any satisfaction to myself."

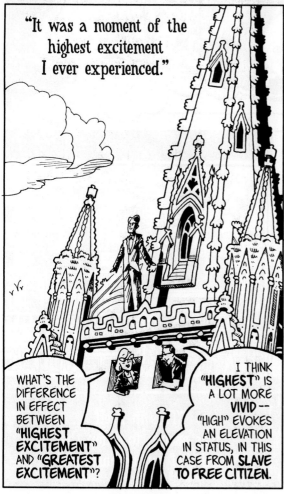

"It was a moment of the highest excitement I ever experienced."

WHAT'S THE DIFFERENCE IN EFFECT BETWEEN "HIGHEST EXCITEMENT" AND "GREATEST EXCITEMENT"?

I THINK "HIGHEST" IS A LOT MORE VIVID -- "HIGH" EVOKES AN ELEVATION IN STATUS, IN THIS CASE FROM SLAVE TO FREE CITIZEN.

"I suppose I felt as one may imagine the unarmed mariner to feel when he is rescued by a friendly man-of-war from the pursuit of a pirate."

"But the loneliness overcame me. There I was in the midst of thousands, and yet a perfect stranger; without home and without friends, in the midst of thousands of my own brethren—children of a common Father...

INTERESTING THAT HE SAYS "BRETHREN" AND "A COMMON **FATHER**" INSTEAD OF "BROTHERS AND SISTERS" OR "A COMMON **MOTHER**"?

IT COULD JUST BE A **GUY** THING.

...LET'S COME BACK TO THAT LATER.

"...and yet I dared not to unfold to any one of them my sad condition. I was afraid to speak to any one for fear of speaking to the wrong one...

"...and thereby falling into the hands of money-loving kidnappers, whose business it was to lie in wait for the panting fugitive...

"...as the ferocious beasts of the forest lie in wait for their prey."

"The motto which I adopted when I started from slavery was this-- 'Trust no man!'"

"I saw in every white man an enemy...

"...and in almost every colored man cause for distrust.

"It was a most painful situation;...

"...and, to understand it, one must needs experience it, or imagine himself in similar circumstances."

"Let him be a fugitive slave in a strange land--

--a land given up to be the hunting-ground for slaveholders--

"whose inhabitants are legalized kidnappers--

--where he is every moment subjected to the terrible liability of being seized upon by his fellowmen,"

"as the hideous crocodile seizes upon his prey!—"

YOU CAN READ DOUGLASS'S BOOK AND SEE IT AS A SEQUENCE OF **IMAGES**--

--A WAY OF **IMAGINING** THE DIFFERENT **SPACES**...

...IN WHICH DOUGLASS EXPERIENCED THE **TRIALS**...

...THAT SHAPED HIS **LIFE**.

YOU CAN ENJOY THE BOOK FOR ITS GRIPPING SCENES...

...AND JUST LET YOURSELF BE TAKEN IN BY DOUGLASS'S HORRIFIC AND MOVING **STORY**...

GASP!

SHH!

FREDERICK DOUGLASS

...OR YOU CAN READ **ACTIVELY** AND TURN YOUR ATTENTION TO PARTICULAR ASPECTS OF DOUGLASS'S **LANGUAGE** OR **LOGIC**.

FOR EXAMPLE...

...YOU MIGHT NOTICE A BIBLICAL ALLUSION TO THE STORY OF **DANIEL** IN THE **LION'S DEN**, WHICH IS FROM THE **OLD TESTAMENT**.

BIB

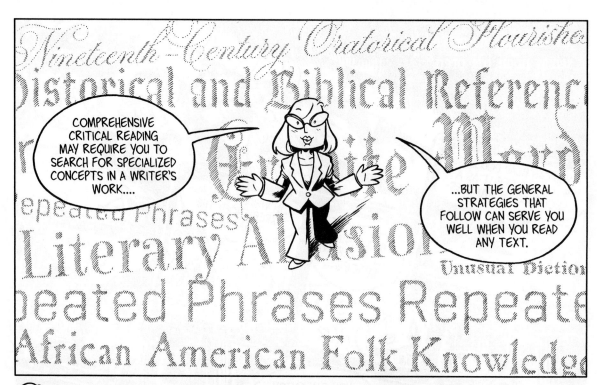

COMPREHENSIVE CRITICAL READING MAY REQUIRE YOU TO SEARCH FOR SPECIALIZED CONCEPTS IN A WRITER'S WORK....

...BUT THE GENERAL STRATEGIES THAT FOLLOW CAN SERVE YOU WELL WHEN YOU READ ANY TEXT.

SOMETIMES YOU ARE CONSIDERING IF THE LANGUAGE IS **EXTREME**.

HYPERBOLE!!! VS. understatement.

SOMETIMES YOU ARE LOOKING FOR INFORMATION THAT THE AUTHOR HAS **OMITTED**.

SOMETIMES YOU ARE LOOKING FOR **UNCLEAR** OR **AMBIGUOUS** LANGUAGE --

-- WHAT IS **DIFFICULT** TO INTERPRET RATHER THAN WHAT IS **EASY**.

PROUST

READING IN THIS WAY...

...IS CALLED **ANALYSIS**.

YOU CAN DO THE **SAME THING** WITH THIS TEXT. SUPPOSE YOU TOOK ALL OF DOUGLASS'S IMAGES OF **WILD ANIMALS** -- AND **WILD MEN** -- FROM THE PASSAGE PRESENTED EARLIER AND **SEPARATED THEM OUT** FROM THE REST OF THE TEXT.

FOCUSING ON THIS KIND OF LANGUAGE WITH **ANIMAL IMAGERY** MIGHT HELP YOU UNDERSTAND THE PREDATORY NATURE OF **SLAVERY**, AND HOW THE INSTITUTION OF SLAVERY TREATS HUMANS LIKE **ANIMALS**.

ABOLITIONIST IMAGERY

OR YOU COULD LOCATE ALL THE TIMES THAT DOUGLASS TALKS ABOUT HOW HE FELT BUT CREATES SOME **SEPARATION** FROM THE EVENTS THAT HE IS RECORDING.

York, I said I felt like
d. I suppose I felt as one ma
imagine the unarmed mariner to feel when
he is rescued by a friendly man-of-war from the pursuit

OFTEN HE DOES THIS BY ADDING MORE **EMOTIONAL DISTANCE** WITH EXTRA VERBS ABOUT **"SAYING"** OR **"SUPPOSING"** IN RELATION TO HIS FEELINGS.

WRITERS SOMETIMES LEAVE **IMPLICIT MESSAGES** IN THEIR TEXTS -- FROM THE LATIN IMPLICARE, MEANING "TO ENFOLD."

WRITE WRITE

FOR EXAMPLE, WHEN DOUGLASS CREATES **SEPARATION** FROM HIM- SELF AND HIS DESCRIPTION OF SLAVERY, HE IS TRYING TO ESTAB- LISH HIMSELF AS AN **OBJECTIVE OBSERVER** OF SLAVERY, NOT JUST A **VICTIM** OF IT.

STUFF STUFF

FREDERICK

THE **IMPLICIT MESSAGE** HERE IS THAT WE CAN **TRUST** DOUGLASS.

ANOTHER WAY TO THINK ABOUT CRITICAL READING IS TO THINK ABOUT IT AS **EXPLICATION**.

to EXPLICATE is to UNFOLD

THE WORD **EXPLICATION** COMES FROM THE LATIN *EXPLICARE*, WHICH MEANS "TO UNFOLD."

EXPLICATION IS THE PROCESS OF **REVEALING** OR **UNCOVERING** IDEAS OR BELIEFS BURIED IN THE TEXT.

DOUGLASS'S PREJUDICES ABOUT CITIES

DOUGLASS'S IDEAS ABOUT THE NATURAL WORLD

DOUGLASS'S ATTITUDES ABOUT AFRICA

THESE IDEAS ARE NOT OBVIOUS; THEY ARE ONLY **SUGGESTED**, PERHAPS **INDIRECTLY**, BY THE TEXT.

FOR INSTANCE, DOUGLASS COMPARES POTENTIAL KIDNAPPERS TO "HIDEOUS CROCODILES."

DOUGLASS WAS WELL AWARE THAT MANY CONSIDERED SLAVES TO BE **ANIMALS**. IN A NICE **REVERSAL**, HIS METAPHOR OF THE CROCODILE IMPLIES THAT **SLAVEHOLDERS** REALLY ARE THE BEASTS.

IF YOU REMEMBER WHAT WE LEARNED ABOUT **PATHOS, LOGOS, ETHOS,** AND **KAIROS** YOU CAN SEE THAT THOSE ARE ALSO AT WORK HERE.

OBVIOUSLY, DOUGLASS IS TRYING TO STIR HIS AUDIENCE'S **EMOTIONS,** BY USING LANGUAGE THAT SUGGESTS THAT **PITY AND FEAR** ARE APPROPRIATE RESPONSES TO HIS TEXT.

THE IMAGES THAT WE MIGHT REMEMBER BEST ARE THE IMAGES OF **EXOTIC SCENES, WILD ANIMALS,** AND **SAVAGE PEOPLES,** WHICH ARE DESIGNED TO EXCITE OUR **EMOTIONS.**

PATHOS

WE CAN ALSO SEE THAT DOUGLASS IS MAKING A NUMBER OF **LOGICAL COMPARISONS** OF SEEMINGLY UNLIKE THINGS.

HE DESCRIBES SLAVE TRADERS AS **BEASTLY**...

...AND HE NOTES THAT ESCAPED SLAVES MIGHT FIND NEW YORK CITY TO BE AS MUCH A PART OF THE SYSTEM OF TERROR AS THE SLAVE-HOLDING **SOUTH**.

HE IS WRITING ABOUT A SUPPOSEDLY CIVILIZED COUNTRY, **AMERICA**, NOT A PLACE LIKE AFRICA, WHICH MANY IN THE UNITED STATES IMAGINED TO BE **VIOLENT** AND **WILD**.

LOGOS

THERE ARE ALSO MANY POINTS IN THIS PASSAGE WHERE DOUGLASS IS CONCERNED WITH HIS **AUTHORITY**, AS A SPEAKER AND WRITER.

HE WAS "**FREQUENTLY ASKED**" HOW HE FELT ABOUT BEING FREE IN NEW YORK, WHICH IMPLIES THAT HIS OPINION WAS SOUGHT BY **MANY**.

ETHOS

83

SYNTHESIS INVOLVES MAKING MEANING FROM MULTIPLE SOURCES.

FOR EXAMPLE, THERE WASN'T JUST **ONE** EDITION OF DOUGLASS'S BOOK.

...THERE WERE **MANY**!

AND, AS DOUGLASS TOLD HIS LIFE STORY, IT GOT A LOT **LONGER**.

THE FIRST VERSION OF HIS BOOK WAS JUST 124 PAGES.

BY THE END OF HIS LIFE, WHEN HE WROTE *THE LIFE AND TIMES OF FREDERICK DOUGLASS*, HIS AUTOBIOGRAPHY HAD GROWN TO OVER **700 PAGES**.

THAT'S A LOT OF MATERIAL TO **SYNTHESIZE**!

THAT'S NOT **ALL**.

THERE WERE ALSO **ILLUSTRATIONS** IN DOUGLASS'S BOOKS THAT WE MIGHT WANT TO **ANALYZE** AND THEN **SYNTHESIZE**.

AFTER ALL, ACCORDING TO **EYEWITNESSES**, THE REAL-LIFE DOUGLASS WAS ABOUT **SIX FEET TALL** AND VERY PHYSICALLY **IMPOSING**.

DOUGLASS WAS DEEPLY CONCERNED ABOUT THE WAY ILLUSTRATIONS IN BOOKS DEPICTED HIM.

BUT WE NEED TO DO SOME MORE **SYNTHESIS** TO PROVE THAT THESIS.

HERE'S A CLUE.

IN 1849 DOUGLASS PRAISED AN **ILLUSTRATED BOOK** ABOUT FAMOUS AFRICAN AMERICANS.

IN THE REVIEW, HE ALSO **RIDICULED** AN ILLUSTRATION OF HIMSELF, WHICH HE SAID HAD A

"much more kindly and amiable expression, than is generally thought to characterize the face of a fugitive slave."

IN 1855 DOUGLASS CAREFULLY CHOSE HIS PORTRAIT FOR THE NEWEST EDITION OF HIS BOOK, AN **ENGRAVING** FROM A **DAGUERREOTYPE** THAT HE HAD POSED FOR.

POOF

BY **ASSEMBLING INFORMATION FROM MULTIPLE SOURCES**, WE CAN REALLY SAY SOMETHING INTERESTING ABOUT A WORK AND HOW TO READ IT CRITICALLY --

-- EVEN ONE THAT PEOPLE THINK THAT THEY ALREADY KNOW **WELL**, LIKE DOUGLASS'S AUTOBIOGRAPHY.

WITH SOMEONE LIKE DOUGLASS THERE MIGHT BE A LOT OF MATERIAL TO SYNTHESIZE.

LET'S GO BACK TO THE **ORIGINAL BOOK** AND ITS 124 PAGES.

YOU CAN DO SYNTHESIS THERE, TOO.

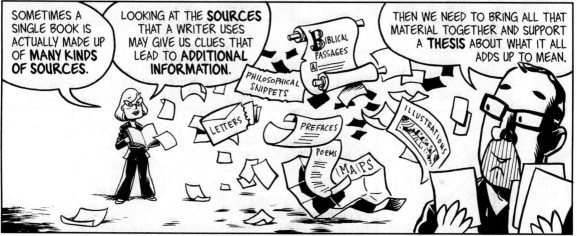

SOMETIMES A SINGLE BOOK IS ACTUALLY MADE UP OF **MANY KINDS** OF SOURCES.

LOOKING AT THE **SOURCES** THAT A WRITER USES MAY GIVE US CLUES THAT LEAD TO **ADDITIONAL INFORMATION**.

THEN WE NEED TO BRING ALL THAT MATERIAL TOGETHER AND SUPPORT A **THESIS** ABOUT WHAT IT ALL ADDS UP TO MEAN.

BIBLICAL PASSAGES

PHILOSOPHICAL SNIPPETS

LETTERS

PREFACES

POEMS

MAPS

ILLUSTRATIONS

BOOKS FROM OUR **OWN** TIME OFTEN CONTAIN A LOT OF DIFFERENT KINDS OF TEXTS **TOO**.

My Life BY A FORMER TEEN POP STAR

A **CELEBRITY BIOGRAPHY** MIGHT INCLUDE **NEWSPAPER STORIES** OR EVEN **BEAUTY TIPS** AND RECIP--!

?!?

SNATCH!

I CAN'T TAKE YOU **ANYWHERE**.

FREDERICK GLASS

WHEN DOUGLASS'S BOOK INITIALLY APPEARED, SOME DOUBTED ITS **AUTHENTICITY**.

THEY THOUGHT THAT FUGITIVE SLAVES **EXAGGERATED** THEIR STORIES OR THAT AFRICAN AMERICANS WEREN'T **LITERATE** ENOUGH TO WRITE ANYTHING DOWN.

THESE PEOPLE THOUGHT THAT ACCOUNTS FROM FUGITIVE SLAVES MUST REALLY BE THE **FICTIONS** OF WHITE **ABOLITIONISTS**.

PROMINENT MEN ATTESTED TO DOUGLASS'S **LITERACY** AND **HONEST CHARACTER** IN LETTERS INCLUDED AT THE FRONT OF HIS BOOK.

THEY WEREN'T **CO-AUTHORS** OF HIS BOOK, BUT THEY WERE **FELLOW WRITERS** IN IT.

DOES THIS MEAN THAT I NEED TO FIND OUT MORE ABOUT **WILLIAM LLOYD GARRISON** AND **WENDELL PHILLIPS**?

THIS IS **WAY TOO MUCH TO SYNTHESIZE** FOR A THREE- TO FIVE-PAGE **PAPER**!

WHEN DOES IT **STOP**?

THE SECRET TO DOING **SYNTHESIS** IS FOCUSING ON **MANAGEABLE** TASKS.

HERE, LET ME GIVE YOU ONE MORE EXAMPLE.

NOT **ANOTHER** EXAMPLE!

RELAX. THIS ONE HAS **PICTURES**.

OKAY.

I LIKE THE EXAMPLES WITH PICTURES.

LET'S TREAT THEM LIKE **PLAYING CARDS** THAT CAN BE SORTED IN THE SAME WAY THAT WE SORT OUT **HEARTS** AND **DIAMONDS** AND **CLUBS** AND **SPADES**.

FOR INSTANCE, WE COULD FIND THE SET OF THREE **VISUAL TEXTS** THAT DEPICT WOMEN AS MAIN CHARACTERS.

WOW.

THOSE THREE IMAGES ARE **REALLY** DIFFERENT.

OR WE COULD FIND THE SET OF PICTURES THAT SHOW DOUGLASS AS AN **ADULT** AT DIFFERENT **STAGES** OF HIS LIFE.

OR WE COULD FIND THE SET OF IMAGES THAT SHOW **WHITE ABOLITIONIST CELEBRITIES.**

BUT **HARRIET BEECHER STOWE** IS ALREADY IN THE "**WOMEN**" SET.

WHEN YOU SORT IMAGES INTO **CATEGORIES**, THE SAME PIECE OF **EVIDENCE** COULD BE SYNTHESIZED WITH MORE THAN ONE POSSIBLE **GROUP.**

YOU CAN DO THE SAME THING WITH **PASSAGES** FROM WRITTEN TEXTS THAT WE JUST DID WITH THESE **ILLUSTRATIONS.**

SOME PEOPLE USE **INDEX CARDS** WITH **QUOTATIONS** FOR THIS PURPOSE.

GREAT!

I'LL WRITE THE **TITLE** OF DOUGLASS'S BOOK ON AN **INDEX CARD.**

LIFE AND TIMES OF FREDERICK DOUGLASS, WRITTEN BY HIMSELF. HIS EARLY LIFE AS A SLAVE, HIS ESCAPE FROM BONDAGE, AND HIS COMPLETE HISTORY TO THE PRESENT TIME, INCLUDING HIS CONNECTION WITH THE SLAVERY MOVEMEN... ROBS IN GREAT B...ELL AS IN HIS OWN ...NY EXPERIE... OF...

THE UNDERGROUND RAILROAD; HIS RELATIONS WITH JOHN BROWN AND THE HARPERS FERRY RAID; HIS RECRUITING THE 54TH AND 55TH MASS. COLORED REGIMENTS; HIS INTERVIEWS WITH PRESIDENTS LINCOLN AND JOHNSON; HIS APPOINTMENT BY G... RANT TO ACCOMPANY THE ...NGO COMMISSION- ...T IN THE COUNCIL ...ET OF C... ...T AS...

HIS APPOINTMENT TO BE RECORDER OF DEEDS IN WASHINGTON BY PRESIDENT J.A. GARFIELD; WITH MANY OTHER INTERESTING AND IMPORTANT EVENTS OF HIS MOST EVENTFUL LIFE; WITH AN INTRODUCTION BY MR. GEORGE L. RUFFIN OF BOSTON. HARTFORD ... PARK PUBLISHING ...RNELL & CO., CL... ...T, SAN J.S. GOODMAN... FRAN...

OR MAYBE **NOT.**

AS I SAID, THE SECRET TO DOING **SYNTHESIS** IS FOCUSING ON MANAGEABLE **TASKS.**

WOW! LOOK HOW FAR WE'VE COME!

THE **AMAZING** THING ABOUT CRITICAL READING IS THAT YOU CAN APPLY THOSE **SAME SKILLS OF ATTENTION** TO **OTHER** CULTURAL OBJECTS THAT YOU ENCOUNTER IN THE WORLD.

YOU CAN "READ" **ADVERTISING** OR **ARCHITECTURE** OR **FASHION** OR **URBAN PLANNING** OR **TRAFFIC PATTERNS.**

CRITICAL READING CAN INVOLVE MANY **KINDS** OF TEXTS, INCLUDING **PAINTINGS, MOVIES,** AND **MUSIC.**

YOU JUST NEED TO KEEP YOUR EYES OPEN AND THINK ABOUT **THE CRITICAL LENSES** THAT YOU WANT TO APPLY TO THEM.

JONATHAN, WHAT DO YOU MEAN BY "CRITICAL LENSES"?

WELL, WHEN YOU READ **CRITICALLY**, YOU MIGHT NOT JUST USE A LENS THAT **MAGNIFIES**.

YOU MAY CHOOSE TO READ A TEXT WITH CRITICAL LENSES THAT DO **DIFFERENT THINGS**.

SOMETIMES YOU MIGHT FIND IT IS INTERESTING TO VIEW A TEXT THROUGH **ANOTHER** TEXT OR PERSPECTIVE.

FOR **EXAMPLE**...

...I MIGHT CHOOSE TO READ A TEXT FROM THE PERSPECTIVE OF **GENDER** -- TO **APPLY** THE CONCEPT OF GENDER TO MY READING OF THE TEXT.

GEND-O-VISION

FOR INSTANCE, I MIGHT ASK HOW DOUGLASS REPRESENTS **FEMALE SLAVES**.

DOES HE DESCRIBE **DIFFERENCES** IN THE TREATMENT OF **MEN** AND **WOMEN** AS SLAVES?

YOU CAN READ A BOOK AS THOUGH YOU ARE READING IT **THROUGH** ANOTHER BOOK--

--**APPLYING** THE IDEAS, PHILOSOPHY, OR METHODS OF ANALYSIS FROM ONE TEXT TO ANOTHER.

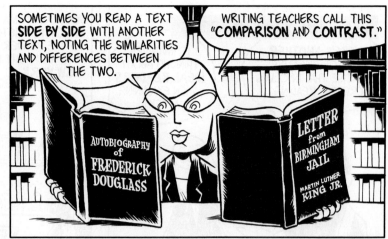

SOMETIMES YOU READ A TEXT **SIDE BY SIDE** WITH ANOTHER TEXT, NOTING THE SIMILARITIES AND DIFFERENCES BETWEEN THE TWO.

WRITING TEACHERS CALL THIS "**COMPARISON** AND **CONTRAST**."

AUTOBIOGRAPHY of FREDERICK DOUGLASS

LETTER from BIRMINGHAM JAIL — MARTIN LUTHER KING JR.

COMPARISON HAS BEEN PART OF RHETORICAL INSTRUCTION SINCE ANCIENT TIMES. IT'S AN IMPORTANT KIND OF **SYNTHESIS** IN CRITICAL READING.

IN **HUMANITIES** CLASSES, ESSAY EXAMINATIONS USUALLY ASK **COMPARISON** AND **CONTRAST** QUESTIONS, BUT THEY SOMETIMES POSE **APPLICATION** QUESTIONS AS WELL.

Compare the text of Douglass's narrative to Olaudah Equiano's slave narrative, which was written many years earlier. Both men were abolitionist speakers who urged the passage of antislavery legislation in the United States and in Great Britain respectively, but they had very different rhetorical techniques. How do they describe captivity and injustice? How do they describe their literacy and public speaking?

Apply W. E. B. DuBois's theory of "double consciousness" to the text of Frederick Douglass's Narrative. In what ways does Douglass seem to experience double consciousness as he interacts with both white and black participants in his story?

WHEN I **COMPARE AND CONTRAST** TWO TEXTS...

...I START BY MAKING LISTS OF HOW THEY'RE ALIKE AND HOW THEY'RE DIFFERENT.

WITH **APPLICATION** QUESTIONS...

...I CAN APPLY THE THEORETICAL TEXTS I'M READING TO NEW **SITUATIONS**.

FOR INSTANCE, I MIGHT APPLY IDEAS FROM **PLATO** AND **ARISTOTLE** TO A GRAPHIC NOVEL I READ FOR A LIT CLASS.

IMAGINING IDEAL READERS

THERE'S **ANOTHER** KIND OF CREATIVE EXERCISE THAT INVOLVES CRITICAL READING.

IT INVOLVES THINKING ABOUT **IDEAL READERS** WHEN EXAMINING A TEXT.

DOUGLASS IS MAKING A VERY **SPECIFIC** RHETORICAL APPEAL TO THE READER TO IDENTIFY WITH HIS PLIGHT IN **NEW YORK**...

...EVEN THOUGH THE SITUATION OF A **FUGITIVE SLAVE** MAY SEEM FAR REMOVED FROM THE CONCERNS OF HIS PRIVILEGED WHITE **AUDIENCES**.

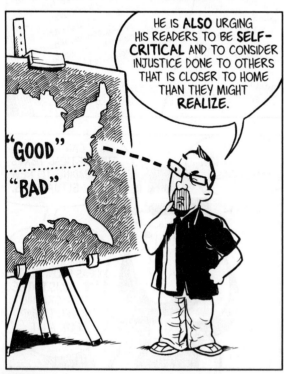

HE IS **ALSO** URGING HIS READERS TO BE **SELF-CRITICAL** AND TO CONSIDER INJUSTICE DONE TO OTHERS THAT IS CLOSER TO HOME THAN THEY MIGHT **REALIZE**.

"GOOD"

"BAD"

TO HELP PERSUADE OTHERS, WRITERS OFTEN IMAGINE AN **IDEAL READER**.

AS HE WROTE, DOUGLASS PROBABLY CONSIDERED HOW A PERSON FROM HIS OWN **TIME** BUT OF A **DIFFERENT RACE** MIGHT READ HIS BOOK.

"I say, let him place himself in my situation—without home or friends—without money or credit—wanting shelter, and no one to give it—wanting bread, and no money to buy it,

"—and at the same time let him feel that he is pursued by merciless men-hunters..."

"—perfectly helpless both as to the means of defence and means of escape,

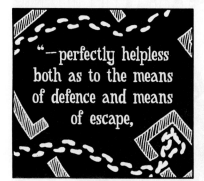

"—in the midst of plenty, yet suffering the terrible gnawings of hunger,—in the midst of houses, yet having no home,

"—among fellow-men, yet feeling as if in the midst of wild beasts, whose greediness to swallow up the trembling and half-famished fugitive is only equalled by that with which the monsters of the deep swallow up the helpless fish upon which they subsist,"

YOUR IDEAL READER FOR THE ESSAYS THAT YOU WRITE IN **COLLEGE** MAY BE VERY MUCH LIKE **YOURSELF**, PARTICULARLY IF YOU ARE PREPARING SOMETHING TO BE READ BY A GROUP OF **PEERS**.

OR YOUR IDEAL READER MIGHT BE MORE OF AN **EXPERT** ON THE SUBJECT TO WHOM YOU WILL WANT TO DEMONSTRATE YOUR **MASTERY** OF THE COURSE MATERIAL.

PEER

YOU

PROFESSOR

PUBLIC

IT IS ALWAYS HELPFUL TO ENVISION A READER **APPROPRIATE** TO A GIVEN PURPOSE AND TO THE PARTICULAR RHETORICAL OCCASION OR **KAIROS**.

YOU MAY THINK YOU DON'T KNOW ENOUGH ABOUT **FREDERICK DOUGLASS** OR THE **PRE-CIVIL WAR PERIOD** IN U.S. HISTORY TO UNDERSTAND WHAT DOUGLASS WANTED READERS TO KNOW.

BUT ANY READER WHO PAYS ATTENTION AND USES SMART READING STRATEGIES CAN LEARN TO EXPLICATE A TEXT AND UNCOVER MEANINGS.

SMART READERS FEEL COMFORTABLE **WRITING** IN THEIR BOOKS.

WHY NOT?

I **PAID** FOR 'EM!

SOMETIMES I USE **SYMBOLS** TO REMIND MYSELF ABOUT IMPORTANT IDEAS.

SOMETIMES I USE MARKERS OF DIFFERENT **COLORS** TO DISTINGUISH BETWEEN DIFFERENT **THEMES**.

OF COURSE, TOO MUCH HIGHLIGHTING ISN'T USEFUL.

IT'S HARD TO DO MUCH **ANALYSIS** IF YOU JUST HAVE A SOLID YELLOW **PAGE**.

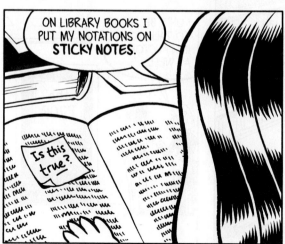

ON LIBRARY BOOKS I PUT MY NOTATIONS ON **STICKY NOTES**.

Is this true?

ON THE INTERNET I PUT **VIRTUAL** STICKY NOTES ON WEB PAGES OR DOCUMENTS.

check w/ study partner!

Reading on the Internet offers opportunities to interact with texts and writers.

Many Web sites offer links to free social bookmarking tools that let you share what you are reading with friends.

thanks! =-)

I'M **CONFUSED** HERE.

WHEN I'M CONFUSED, SOMETIMES I LOOK THINGS UP ON THE WEB.

AND YOU'LL NEED TO EVALUATE THE SOURCE NO MATTER **WHERE** YOU FIND IT.

BUT IT IS TRUE THAT IF YOU ARE GOING TO USE THE MATERIAL FROM THE WEB IN A **WRITING ASSIGNMENT**, YOU SHOULD CHECK TO SEE IF IT COMES FROM A RELIABLE **SOURCE*** --

-- A SOURCE WRITTEN BY **RECOGNIZED EXPERTS** WITH THE AUTHORITY TO SPEAK OR WRITE ABOUT AN ISSUE.

* For more on research, see CHAPTER 6.

DON'T BE AFRAID TO TALK TO YOUR INSTRUCTORS AS WELL.

the PROF

YOU CAN **ALSO** ASK OTHER PEOPLE FOR HELP WITH A DIFFICULT PASSAGE.

TRADITIONALLY, READING HAS BEEN A SOCIAL PROCESS IN WHICH WE SHARE OUR EXPERIENCES OF READING WITH **OTHERS.**

IN THE EIGHTEENTH AND NINE-TEENTH **CENTURIES,** PEOPLE OFTEN SHARED **BOOKS** AND **NEWSPAPERS** WITH FRIENDS, AND FAMILIES READ **OUT LOUD** TOGETHER EACH NIGHT.

SOME **LITERACY SPECIALISTS** SAY THAT EVEN TODAY READING ALOUD ISN'T JUST FOR **KIDS.**

THE MORE THAT STUDENTS UNDERSTAND THAT READING IS A **PUBLIC** AND **SOCIAL ACTIVITY,** THE MORE THEY **IMPROVE.**

SOMETIMES I NEED TO GO OVER A PAGE MORE THAN **ONCE.**

GOOD READERS AREN'T NECESSARILY **FAST** READERS.

AND YOU MIGHT SEE SOMETHING IN A TEXT THAT ANOTHER STUDENT **DOESN'T** SEE.

THANKS, I THINK THAT --

WOW!

SEE?

REFRAME with Luis & Cindy

How do I READ this?

beep beep boop

bleep-a-bloop!

ARE YOU STILL UP?

YES, I'M FINISHING UP SOME OF THE READING.

ME TOO, I'M REALLY **BEHIND**. WHEN I WENT HOME FOR MY BROTHER'S SEND-OFF, IT WAS HARD TO FIND ANY TIME FOR **SCHOOLWORK**. IT WAS NEVER REALLY QUIET ENOUGH TO CONCENTRATE.

WHEN I CAME BACK FROM MY TRIP, I FIGURED THAT THESE WERE JUST COMIC BOOKS AND THAT I COULD SPEED-READ THEM, BUT THIS IS TAKING **FOREVER**.

YEAH, COMIC BOOKS AREN'T ALWAYS A QUICK READ.

I'VE BEEN READING THE GRAPHIC ADAPTATION OF **THE 9/11 REPORT** FOR MY CLASS.

DO YOU HAVE TO ANALYZE THE **WORDS** OR THE **IMAGES** OR **BOTH**?

THAT'S THE TRICKY PART, LUIS. ANALYZING **IMAGES** IS TOUGHER THAN I THOUGHT. BUT I FEEL PRETTY CONFIDENT TALKING ABOUT THE **WRITTEN** TEXT.

graphic novel adaptation

original report

AFTER ALL, THE INFORMATION COMES STRAIGHT FROM THE **ACTUAL REPORT** OF THE 9/11 COMMISSION.

SOME OF THE LANGUAGE IS EVEN THE SAME, **WORD-FOR-WORD**, LIKE THE TITLES OF THE CHAPTERS.

I'M THINKING OF COMPARING THE TWO SOURCES IN MY ESSAY.

EVEN BEFORE THEY TURNED IT INTO A COMIC, PARTS OF THE ORIGINAL REPORT READ MORE LIKE A **THRILLER** THAN A DRY LEGAL DOCUMENT.

SOME OF THE SECTIONS EVEN HAVE SUSPENSE-FUL TITLES:

1 "WE HAVE SOME PLANES"

8 "THE SYSTEM WAS BLINKING RED"

I GUESS THE WRITERS OF THE **GOVERNMENT REPORT** REALLY WANTED TO GRAB PEOPLE'S ATTENTION BY DRAMATICALLY SETTING THE **SCENE**.

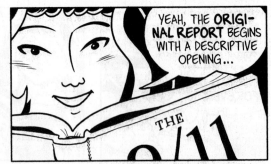

YEAH, THE **ORIGINAL REPORT** BEGINS WITH A DESCRIPTIVE OPENING...

"TUESDAY, SEPTEMBER 11, 2001, dawned temperate and nearly cloudless in the eastern United States."

"Millions of men and women readied themselves for work."

"Some made their way to the Twin Towers, the signature structures of the World Trade Center complex in New York City."

"Others went to Arlington, Virginia, to the Pentagon."

"Across the Potomac River, the United States Congress was back in session."

"At the other end of Pennsylvania Avenue, people began to line up for a White House Tour."

"In Sarasota, Florida, President George W. Bush went for an early morning run."

THAT'S A LOT LIKE THE SECTION I JUST READ ABOUT "**STRATEGIC READING**." FREDERICK DOUGLASS ALSO USED **VERBAL PICTURES** TO MAKE HIS ARGUMENT MORE **ENGAGING** AND **CONVINCING**.

BUT **READING CRITICALLY** MEANS MORE THAN JUST IMAGINING YOURSELF IN THE SCENE.

YOU HAVE TO ANALYZE THE **CHOICE** OF INDIVIDUAL ELEMENTS IN THE TEXT AND HOW THEY FIT TOGETHER IN WAYS THAT MIGHT NOT BE IMMEDIATELY **OBVIOUS**.

THAT SOUNDS LIKE MUCH LESS OF A **THRILLER**.

WELL, THERE'S STILL SOMETHING SATISFYING ABOUT ASSEMBLING ALL THOSE CLUES. I MEAN, LOOK BACK AT THAT OPENING.

THE FIRST SENTENCE IS UP IN THE **CLOUDLESS SKY**.

BUT THE SECOND TAKES PLACE DOWN ON THE GROUND AT THE **HUMAN LEVEL**.

THE THIRD SENTENCE IS ABOUT THE **PRIVATE SECTOR**, AND THE FOURTH IS ABOUT THE **MILITARY**, ALTHOUGH THEY BOTH DISCUSS DAILY COMMUTERS ON THE **MOVE**.

AND THE REST OF THE OPENING IS ABOUT THE PEOPLE WHO MIGHT BE ULTIMATELY RESPONSIBLE FOR PREVENTING **ANOTHER** TERRORIST ATTACK: THE **LEGISLATIVE** AND **EXECUTIVE** BRANCHES OF **GOVERNMENT**.

"*TUESDAY, SEPTEMBER 11, 2001, dawned temperate and nearly cloudless in the eastern United States.*"

"*Some made their way to the Twin Towers, the signature structures of the World Trade Center complex in New York City.*"

"*Across the Potomac River, the United States Congress was back in session.*"

"*At the other end of Pennsylvania Avenue, people began to line up for a White House Tour.*"

"*In Sarasota, Florida, President George W. Bush went for an early morning run.*"

IN THE **GRAPHIC NOVEL**, THE FIRST SENTENCE FOCUSES DIRECTLY ON THE PLANES.

"BEFORE 8 O'CLOCK ON TUESDAY, SEPTEMBER 11, 2001, A PLEASANT AND CLOUDLESS MORNING IN BOSTON, TWO PLANES, BOTH BOEING 767S, WERE ABOUT TO TAKE OFF FROM LOGAN AIRPORT."

SO WHEN YOU LOOK CLOSELY AT THE **LANGUAGE** AND THE **LOGIC** OF A PASSAGE, YOU CAN ACTUALLY SEE **IMPLICIT ARGUMENTS** THERE.

RIGHT. BUT YOU HAVE TO **EXPLICATE** THEM.

OR **UNFOLD** THEM.

UNFOLD

READING THE **WORDS** IS EASY. I DON'T KNOW WHAT TO SAY ABOUT READING THE PICTURES.

?

KNOCK KNOCK!

UH...

...LUIS, I'LL HAVE TO CALL YOU BACK.

WHAT'S INTERESTING IS HOW MUCH **BLACK** THE COMIC INCLUDES.

THEY EMPHASIZE THE SERIOUS, SOBER QUALITY OF THE EVENT BY USING THE COLOR BLACK, A COLOR TRADITIONALLY ASSOCIATED WITH **MOURNING** IN OUR COUNTRY.

WE'RE FINALLY OFF, LADIES AND GENTLEMEN.

THANKS FOR THE **TIPS**!

BLACK ALSO FOCUSES THE READER'S ATTENTION ON HOW MANY THINGS THAT HAPPENED IN THE HIJACKINGS ARE STILL **UNKNOWN**, BECAUSE INVESTIGATORS ARE STILL "IN THE DARK" ABOUT EXACTLY WHAT TOOK **PLACE**.

Beep Beep Beep

HEY, LUIS, I HAVE SOMETHING TO **SHOW** YOU...

...AND THEN I HAVE TO GET BACK TO **READING**.

COMING UP IN THE NEXT EXCITING EPISODE OF **REFRAME** →

"Am I having an IDENTITY CRISIS?"

[pg. 141]

"CLOSE READING"

1 why READ CLOSELY?

CLOSE READING ISN'T JUST FOR LITERARY TEXTS. DOCUMENTS YOU ENCOUNTER IN SCHOOL, PROFESSIONAL, AND PRIVATE LIFE ALSO CALL FOR CLOSE READING.

LOOK AT THIS DOCUMENT ABOUT POLICIES FOR MONITORING COMPUTER USE, WHICH COMES FROM A COLLEGE WEB SITE.

Under normal circumstances, college officials will not examine personal information transmitted over the network or stored on college-owned computers. However, the college reserves the right to monitor system resources, including activity and accounts, with or without notice, when:

1 It is necessary to protect the integrity, security, or functionality of college computing resources.

2 An account or system is engaged in unusual or excessive activity.

3 It has good cause to believe that regulations, rules, or laws are being violated.

4 In the event of health, safety, or security emergencies, as determined by authorized college officials.

Additionally, the normal operation and maintenance of the college's computing resources requires the backup of data, the logging of activity, the monitoring of general usage patterns, and other such activities as may be necessary in order to provide desired services.

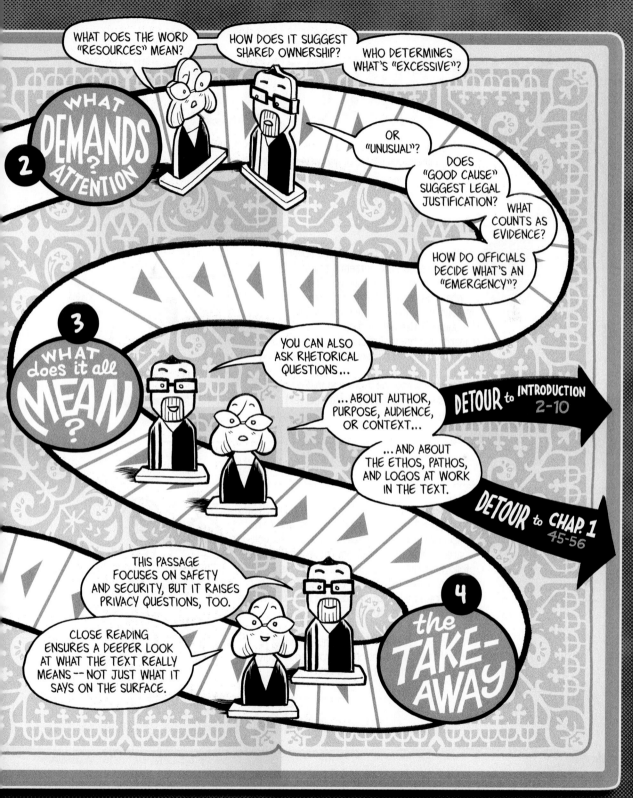

DRAWING CONCLUSIONS

The activities below ask you to focus on the rhetorical dimensions of texts and visuals you might write about.

1 Choose one print text and one nonprint text that you are currently reading. Consider all of the ways you "notate" what you read, either in writing or in your head. Do you make real notes? Use stickies? Use digital stickies? If you primarily use "mental stickies," what kinds of questions do you ask about what you read?

Write down some questions you might ask, or notes you might make, about the texts you have chosen.

2 Consider how you might use some terms from Chapter 1 -- *logos, ethos, pathos,* and *kairos* -- to engage in active reading. Pick a work you are reading for a class and make a note of the following: the subject, how the text builds logos, how the writer establishes ethos, how the text demonstrates a use of pathos, and how the writer shows an awareness of kairos.

What do you discover? How might attending to these rhetorical dimensions improve your ability to read -- and summarize -- a text?

3 Choose a text that you might be called upon to analyze, such as a journal article, a work of art, or a video or film. Make a list of all of the questions you have about it, as well as all of the points that you find interesting.

Next, make a list of quotations, still images, characteristics of the work, or other information that has popped out at you during your reading of the text.

Now group these pieces according to criteria that make sense to you, as Liz does with the images from Frederick Douglass's autobiography on pp. 91-93. Consider the questions you listed in light of your arrangement of pieces from the text. Rearrange questions and textual evidence as needed. What new insights emerge for you from this process?

4 Think about the book you're reading right now -- *Understanding Rhetoric.* Look back at the discussion on pp. 87-88 of Frederick Douglass's interest in controlling the way he appeared in images in print. Why do you think that this book uses Douglass as an example? What evidence do you find that indicates that the writers and illustrators of this book thought carefully about the images it includes? What choices might you have made differently?

RHETORIC IS ABOUT PRESENTING A CHARACTER THAT AN AUDIENCE WILL **TRUST**....

... AND ABOUT BOTH INSPIRING **PASSIONATE EMOTIONS** AND STRUCTURING **RATIONAL ARGUMENTS**.

RHETORIC IS ALSO ABOUT SAYING THE RIGHT THING AT THE RIGHT TIME.

UH... L-LIZ?

IT'S, UH... UM.

YIKES!

WHAT WAS **THAT?**

AAH!

PHONE

ZOOOM!!!

HOLD ON!

IF I WANTED TO PRESENT SOME SCIENTIFIC INFORMATION--

--SAY, IN A DISCUSSION OF THE MOLECULAR STRUCTURE OF MY SUPER-SUIT--

--I'D PRESENT IT CAREFULLY AND OBJECTIVELY, THE WAY A **SCIENTIST** WOULD!

BUT IF WE PUT ON OTHER COSTUMES, IT DOESN'T REALLY CHANGE WHO WE ARE.

...

PUTTING ON A KNIGHT'S COSTUME DOESN'T MAKE ME HEROIC.

NO, BUT SOCIAL CONTEXTS MATTER, AND MOST PEOPLE WEAR A LOT OF DIFFERENT COSTUMES FOR THEIR DIFFERENT SOCIAL ROLES.

CHANGING YOUR IDENTITY MAY BE ABOUT CHOOSING THE RIGHT FRAME OF MIND.

OH, I GET IT.

THIS IS AN OUTFIT I **TEACH** IN.

I DON'T REALLY WEAR IT AROUND THE **HOUSE**.

STANDING UP IN FRONT OF A CLASS SOUNDS PRETTY HEROIC TO **ME**.

A LOT OF PEOPLE TREAT PROFESSIONAL CLOTHING AS A KIND OF **ARMOR**.

IT GIVES THEM **AUTHORITY** AND MAKES THEM FEEL LESS **VULNERABLE**.

LIKEWISE, T-SHIRTS OFTEN MAKE CLEAR **RHETORICAL STATEMENTS**.

RUSTLE RUSTLE

FOR EXAMPLE, WEARING A T-SHIRT FROM A *STAR TREK* CONVENTION MIGHT SHOW THAT SOMEONE IS A BIG FAN.

LIVE LONG & PROSPER

THIS ONE IS FROM A VIDEO-GAME CONFERENCE, WHERE I GAVE A TALK ABOUT EDUCATIONAL GAMES.

GDC

SO ONE T-SHIRT IS ABOUT EXPRESSING YOUR ROLE AS A FAN, AND THE OTHER IS ABOUT YOUR ROLE AS AN ESTABLISHED EXPERT.

HERE'S A DRESS THAT I WORE WHEN I WAS A SUNDAY SCHOOL TEACHER.

MY STUDENTS EXPECTED ME TO BE FORMAL AND RESPECTABLE.

AND HERE ARE EXERCISE CLOTHES THAT I WEAR TO GYM CLASS WHEN I KNOW NOBODY'S LOOKING AT ME.

SOUNDS LIKE YOU HAVE A LOT OF DIFFERENT SOCIAL ROLES.

IN SOME ROLES YOU'RE A TEACHER, AND IN SOME YOU'RE A STUDENT.

SO YOU ALSO HAVE DIFFERENT LEVELS OF AUTHORITY.

127

AWESOME! THAT'S MY BOSS'S **CALL SIGN**.

IT MEANS SHE'LL BE **FIGHTING CRIME** ALL NIGHT, SO I GET THE EVENING OFF!

C'MON -- I WANT TO SHOW YOU SOMETHING **COOL**!

METACRAFT

?

Y'KNOW...

...PRETENDING CAN BE AN IMPORTANT PART OF WHAT WE CALL

INVENTION...

to SECRET **INTERN** HIDEOUT

...THAT IS, PLAYING DIFFERENT ROLES TO EXPLORE DIFFERENT SITUATIONS, DIFFERENT IDEAS, AND DIFFERENT CIRCUMSTANCES WE MIGHT WANT TO WRITE ABOUT.

INTERNS' CAVE

SECRET! NO BOSSES ALLOWED!

DO NOT ENTER

INTERNS ONLY!

NO SOLICITORS

I HOPE TO BECOME A HARDWORKING SUPERHERO, BUT SINCE I'M A RECENT COLLEGE GRADUATE, I COULD ONLY GET SUPERCON TO TAKE ME ON AS AN **UNPAID INTERN**.

IT'S TIME TO USE MY SUPERHERO POWERS OF **DISCOURSE** TO SAVE THE DAY !

ALL THE OTHER SUPERHERO INTERNS HAVE BEEN TALKING ABOUT HOW TO HANDLE THE SITUATION -- BUT THEIR TONE NEEDS SOME WORK.

HERE'S A VIDEO FROM OUR LAST SECRET MEETING.....

DOOP.

PLAY

SUPERCONGLOMERATE'S TREATMENT OF SUPERHERO INTERNS IS REPREHENSIBLE.

SUPERCON'S BIGWIGS ARE TREATING US LIKE SLAVES!

133

ALL OF US SUPERHEROES PERFORM COMPLEX TASKS -- DRAWING ON WHAT WE LEARNED IN COLLEGE.

BUT EVERY JOB REQUIRES THE LEARNING OF NEW SKILLS. AN INTERNSHIP CAN BE AN IMPORTANT BRIDGE BETWEEN COLLEGE AND CAREER.

IS IT FAIR, THOUGH, TO REQUIRE ON-THE-JOB TRAINING WITHOUT COMPENSATION?

YOUR **TONE** SHOULD ENGAGE YOUR AUDIENCE IN A WAY THAT WILL INVITE THEM TO FEEL RECEPTIVE TO YOUR MESSAGE.

AND YOUR **VOICE** -- YOUR IDENTITY AS A WRITER -- SHOULD PROJECT THE APPROPRIATE KIND OF AUTHORITY AND AGENCY.

RECORDING BOOTH

EXACTLY!

I ALWAYS NEED TO THINK ABOUT THE AUDIENCE I'M TRYING TO REACH IN MY RHETORICAL SITUATION -- AND MAKE SURE I ADJUST MY TONE AND VOICE TO GET THE EFFECT I WANT.

AHEM.

"INCLUDING SUPERHERO INTERNS IN THE SUPERCON COMPENSATION PLAN IS THE RIGHT THING TO DO. TREATING INTERNS AS PROFESSIONAL WORKERS WILL IMPROVE CUSTOMER SERVICE AND ATTRACT BETTER TALENT TO THE FIELD."

UM, METAMORPH -- THAT WOULD BE GREAT, EXCEPT FOR ONE THING.

YES.

ACCORDING TO THIS SCHEDULE, YOU ARE SUPPOSED TO BE RECORDING A PODCAST FOR HIGH SCHOOL STUDENTS CONSIDERING A VOCATIONAL TRACK IN SUPERHERODOM.

OOPS.

I MUST HAVE MIXED UP MY NOTES.

THE IDENTITY YOU PROJECT NEEDS TO CONVEY YOUR **ETHOS**, YOUR SENSE OF **CREDIBILITY**, FOR THE AUDIENCE YOU'RE ADDRESSING.

SO LET'S TRY THAT ONE AGAIN.

"BEING A SUPER-HERO INTERN MEANS YOU GET TO PLAY WITH A LOT OF

AWESOME GEAR!

BUT CHECK OUT WHAT FORMER INTERNS HAVE SAID ABOUT SUPERCONGLOMERATE ON SOCIAL MEDIA TO SEE IF YOU'LL GET ENOUGH OUT OF YOUR INTERNSHIP TO JUSTIFY WEEKS OF WORK WITHOUT PAY..."

THAT'S BETTER!

YOU'RE DEMONSTRATING AN **ETHOS** THAT THIS AUDIENCE CAN APPRECIATE.

WHEN YOU TRIED SPECIFI-CALLY TO REACH A YOUNGER AUDIENCE, YOU CREATED A COMPLETELY **DIFFERENT** RHETORICAL EFFECT.

WELL, I **DO** HAVE SUPERPOWERS OF DISCOURSE.

THAT'S TRUE -- BUT USING DIFFERENT VOICES IN THAT WAY IS A SKILL THAT ANYONE CAN LEARN WITH ENOUGH PRACTICE.

KEEP IN MIND THE VARIOUS FACTORS THAT GO INTO PERFORMANCE AND WHAT EFFECT THEY HAVE...

IDENTITY

ADOPTING A DISGUISE

RECOGNIZABLE INDIVIDUAL

ORDINARY PERSON

data

evidence

TONE

POLARIZING | PASSIONATE

NEUTRAL | DISENGAGED

VOICE

Familiarity | Formality

PERSONAL | MANNERED

IMPERSONAL | CONVERSATIONAL

PERFORMANCE →

139

THE MOST IMPORTANT THING TO REMEMBER IS THAT IF YOUR PERFORMANCE OF ONE IDENTITY DOESN'T GO PERFECTLY, YOU CAN STILL TAKE ADVANTAGE OF THE LEARNING EXPERIENCE IT OFFERS.

THAT'S EASY FOR YOU TO SAY!

AHEM!

YOU CAN USE CRITICAL COMMENTS TO MAKE SUBSTANTIVE CHANGES IN YOUR RHETORICAL STYLE.

REMEMBER, PRESENTING AN IDENTITY EFFECTIVELY TAKES PRACTICE!

REFRAME with Luis & Cindy

Am I having an IDENTITY CRISIS?

SNAP!!

UGH.

LIBRARY STUDY ROOM

SNAP!

UGH!

CINDY?

CINDY, WHAT'S UP?

LUIS, HELP! I'M HAVING AN IDENTITY CRISIS.

I'M SUPPOSED TO WRITE AN ETHNOGRAPHY. BUT I'M NOT REALLY SURE WHAT THAT IS.

UGH.

WHY DID I PRETEND TO UNDERSTAND THE ASSIGNMENT?

HMM... ASKING QUESTIONS MIGHT NOT BE PART OF YOUR IDENTITY.

I'D SUGGEST A PERSONALITY TRANSPLANT.

VERY FUNNY. HOW ABOUT GIVING ME SOME HELP?

HERE, LET ME SHOW YOU THE ASSIGNMENT.

FLIP OPEN

ASSIGNMENT

One of your goals for this class is to observe and understand the complexities and nuances of online communities. In preparation for your final digital ethnography project, you'll select an online community to which you currently belong and that you can closely observe and interact with for several weeks. Participating with the group will be part of how you will understand its norms.

I'M ONLINE EVERY DAY--

SMILE!

SNAP!

I CHECK SOCIAL NETWORK SITES, BROWSE PROFILES, PARTICIPATE IN DISCUSSIONS...

TYPE TYPE

...BUT I'VE NEVER WRITTEN AN **ETHNO-GRAPHY** BEFORE!

UPLOAD

HMM...

WELL, "ETHNO" MEANS A GROUP OF PEOPLE, AND "GRAPH" MEANS WRITING.

SO "ETHNOGRAPHY" IS JUST **WRITING ABOUT PEOPLE.**

I THINK IT'S MORE COMPLICATED THAN THAT, LUIS.

WE'RE STUDYING **ONLINE COMMUNITIES.** WE'RE SUPPOSED TO FOCUS ON GROUPS OF PEOPLE WITH **COMMON INTERESTS** WHO USE THE INTERNET AS THEIR **MAIN** METHOD OF COMMUNICATION.

AN ONLINE COMMUNITY FOSTERS IDENTIFI-CATION WITH A GROUP OF PEOPLE WITH SIMILAR INTERESTS OR OBJECTIVES.

MEMBERS SHARE A COMMITMENT TO VALUES HELD IN COMMON AND OFTEN SHARE LABOR AND LEADERSHIP.

COOL, I HAVE THAT ASSIGNMENT, TOO. MY PROFESSOR SAYS WE'RE SUPPOSED TO OBSERVE A GROUP AND WRITE DOWN EVERYTHING WE SEE AND HEAR.

WE'RE EXPLORING OUR IDENTITIES AS RESEARCHERS.

I DECIDED TO WRITE ABOUT VIDEO GAMES AND THE FRIENDS I'VE MADE ONLINE. GAMING HAS BEEN PART OF MY DAILY LIFE SINCE HIGH SCHOOL. IT'S A WAY TO KEEP IN TOUCH WITH OLD FRIENDS...

...AND IT HELPS ME MEET NEW PEOPLE, TOO.

IDENTITY

OF COURSE, WHEN YOU ARE WRITING ABOUT FRIENDS THAT YOU CARE ABOUT...

ADOPTING DISGUISE

RECOGNIZABLE INDIVIDUAL

...IT'S IMPORTANT TO BE **YOURSELF** AND PRESENT YOUR EXPERTISE **HONESTLY.**

ORDINARY PERSON

JUST AS YOU TELL THE TRUTH ABOUT THE SUBJECTS YOU OBSERVE.

REPORT YOUR OBSERVATIONS.

ARGH!

LIBRARY STUDY ROOM

THIS ASSIGNMENT IS **EASY** FOR YOU. WHAT ABOUT **ME**?

I'M AN ENGINEERING STUDENT. WHEN DO I HAVE TIME FOR ONLINE COMMUNITIES? POSTING RANDOM SELFIES IS ABOUT ALL THAT I CAN DO.

DUE! waaaay 2 much work

nagging again

ENGINEE vol.3 but I do luv it ♥♥

HMM... WHAT ABOUT THE STUDENT ENGINEERING CLUB? THAT'S A COMMUNITY YOU CARE ABOUT. YOU **IDENTIFY** WITH THEM.

HEY, I HAVE AN **IDEA**!

LAST WEEK I WAS MAKING A POSTER FOR THE CLUB AND SEARCHING ONLINE FOR SOME IMAGES TO USE...

Search Results for "engineer"

...AND I REALIZED THAT MOST OF THE IMAGES ON THE INTERNET OF WHAT AN ENGINEER LOOKS LIKE DON'T LOOK **ANYTHING LIKE ME**!

NO. I DON'T SEE YOU IN A HARD HAT.

COMING UP IN THE NEXT EXCITING EPISODE OF **REFRAME**

"The OFFICE hour!"

[pg. 181]

WALK the TALK

"IDENTITIES"

1 Who is the WRITER HERE?

> READERS FORM AN IMPRESSION OF YOU FROM THE IDENTITIES YOU PROJECT IN WRITING. THINK ABOUT HOW YOU CAN PRESENT YOURSELF MOST EFFECTIVELY.

> A LINKEDIN PAGE SHOWCASES A WRITER'S IDENTITY AS A PROFESSIONAL, SO YOUR GOAL ON LINKEDIN IS TO PROJECT YOUR BEST SELF FOR THE KIND OF WORK YOU WANT TO DO.

 in   Search for people, jobs, companies, and more... 🔍

Background

 Summary

My name is Uzair Mohammad, and I'm seeking to apply my engineering experience to develop and create novel devices and tools, and to build a career with an organization seeking experience in engineering design, project management, enthusiastic leadership, excellent communication, and creativity in problem solving.

-Bioengineer with 5+ years of project management experience in bioengineering and biotechnology
-Driven team leader, founder of engineering startup with novel "Biofiltration" microfilter technology
-Practiced communicator, presented TED Talk on "Biofiltration" Technology (TEDxUCSD 2014)
-Experienced with legal scientific notebooks, and science/engineering report writing, grants, and patents.
-Recognized and Awarded by US Air Force, US Navy, Lawrence Livermore National Labs, IEEE, The National Science Foundation, and Brown University for excellence in Engineering and Communication.

Courtesy Uzair Mohammad

DRAWING CONCLUSIONS

The following assignments ask you to think about
the importance of identity when composing.

1 This chapter mentions Barbara Ehrenreich's
Nickel and Dimed, a book about the struggles
of the working poor that relies on the author's
experience of getting by on minimum-wage jobs.

What personal experiences have you had that
connect you to an idea or a subject that interests
you? How can you use your experiences to explore
that subject in a piece of writing? Draft a proposal
for a writing project in a genre of your choosing
(perhaps a Web essay or a newspaper editorial)
that uses your firsthand experience to enhance
the discussion of your topic.

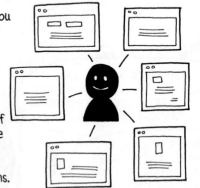

2 Keep notes for a week about how you
interact with others through various
online sites. How do you represent
yourself -- in filling out required or
requested information, in uploading
content, and in interacting with others?

Write a short autoethnography -- a brief
narrative describing your own use of the
sites -- that analyzes your experiences
and discusses how you use different
identities in different rhetorical situations.

3

Look at pp. 133-35 of this chapter, in which extreme and bland tones are represented both verbally and visually. Choose a short text, such as an email or online posting, that you have written in the past month with a particular audience in mind.

Who is the audience? What tone do you take in your writing? Turn your original text into an audience-appropriate media text (perhaps a comic, collage, poster, or video) that uses visuals or other nonverbal means to help convey tone.

4

Many students feel anxiety about public speaking and presenting their ideas in front of large groups of people. What is the largest audience that you have ever had to address? How did you prepare for your presentation?

Looking back, what worked well, and what should you have done differently? How did the composition of the audience affect how you felt about your performance?

Issue 4 • Argument Beyond Pro and Con

SETTING THE SCENE FOR ARGUABLE ASSERTIONS

JUST LIKE IN THE ERA OF CLASSICAL RHETORIC, SPEAKERS ARE ALWAYS POINTING OUT HOW CIRCUMSTANCES **HAVE** CHANGED...

...**ARE** CHANGING...

...OR ARE **LIKELY** TO CHANGE.

AND THESE CHANGES MIGHT BE FOR THE WORSE OR FOR THE **BETTER**...

...AND THEY MIGHT BE GRADUAL "EVOLUTIONS" OR DRAMATIC "REVOLUTIONS"!

EXCUSE ME!

HEY, IF YOU REALLY WANT TO TALK ABOUT ARGUMENT, MAYBE YOU NEED A **TALK SHOW HOST!**

WHO INVITED **YOU** HERE?

THIS IS A PRIVATE CONVERSATION!

THIS DOESN'T LOOK LIKE A VERY **PRIVATE** CONVERSATION TO **ME.**

UH... RIGHT.

I GUESS WE **ARE** CHARACTERS IN A **BOOK.**

OKAY THEN...

K-CHONK!

A GOOD **ARGUMENT** IS ACTUALLY A LOT LIKE A GOOD **CONVERSATION.**

IT'S IMPORTANT TO REPRESENT **MORE** THAN ONE SIDE.

WHA--!

HUH?

GOOD POINT! IN A WAY, TALK SHOWS STAGE DEBATES AS CONVERSATIONS AMONG SEVERAL DIFFERENT PARTICIPANTS.

WHEW! GUESTS ON TALK SHOWS SOMETIMES INSIST THAT ONLY **THEIR** SIDE CAN BE RIGHT, AND THE OTHER SIDE IS NECESSARILY **WRONG**, AND THEY NEVER CONCEDE **ANYTHING** TO THEIR OPPONENTS.

CON

PLEASE, MA'AM -- A GOOD ARGUMENT HAS TO GET BEYOND PRO AND CON DEBATES BETWEEN OVERSIMPLIFIED **OPPOSITES!**

RRGH! SIR!

COMPLEX CONVERSATIONS AREN'T JUST ABOUT **RIGHT** AND **WRONG!**

KICK!

POINT ACCUSINGLY!

NO! YES! NO!! PRO

IN THE DEBATE ABOUT **IMMIGRATION,** FOR INSTANCE, PARTICIPANTS ARE ACTUALLY ARGUING ABOUT THEIR VALUES AND THE DIFFERENT VISIONS THEY HAVE FOR THE COUNTRY.

VIEWED THAT WAY, THE DEBATE ABOUT IMMIGRATION ISN'T JUST ABOUT WHETHER TO LET IMMIGRANTS IN OR NOT. IT'S ALSO ABOUT HOW WE WANT TO DEFINE WHAT AMERICA IS.

MAYFLOWER

NO NO NO CON

KICK 'EM OUT!

PRO YES LET TH

THINKING ABOUT WHAT'S REALLY AT STAKE IN ANY GIVEN DEBATE REVEALS THE ARGUMENT'S **ASSERTIONS,** OR THE PARTICULAR CLAIMS BEING MADE.

A STATEMENT IS **ARGUABLE** IF IT REPRESENTS A POSITION WITH WHICH A REASONABLE PERSON COULD DISAGREE.

FOR INSTANCE, CONSIDER CHILDREN BROUGHT TO THIS COUNTRY **ILLEGALLY** BY THEIR PARENTS WHEN THEY WERE TOO YOUNG TO GIVE **CONSENT.**

BEFORE

COLLEGE

AFTER

SHOULD SUCH CHILDREN BE TREATED AS **"CRIMINALS"**? SHOULD THEY, FOR EXAMPLE, BE DENIED THE RIGHT TO ATTEND AMERICAN UNIVERSITIES?

LET'S CONSIDER THE EVIDENCE IN A LESS COMPLEX CASE.

IT LOOKS LIKE A BREAK-IN...

...BUT WAS IT?

BREAKING INTO A CABIN THAT DOESN'T BELONG TO YOU MIGHT NOT BE THE WRONG THING TO DO...

B.B.

...IF YOU'RE IN AN EMERGENCY SITUATION...

B.B.

...AND **IF** THE BREAK-IN COULD PREVENT SOMETHING WORSE FROM HAPPENING.

A LOT DEPENDS ON WHAT HAPPENED BEFORE THE BREAK-IN AND ON WHAT HAPPENED AFTERWARD.

HOME SWEET HOME

Papa B.

A

Mama B.

B

Baby B.

C

AND A LOT DEPENDS ON WHO IS LOOKING AT THE INCIDENT.

THE OWNER OF THIS CABIN AND THE PERSON WHO BREAKS IN MIGHT SEE THE SITUATION VERY DIFFERENTLY.

ZOOMING IN ON CLAIMS AND EVIDENCE

AN ARGUMENT NEEDS **GROUNDS** OR **EVIDENCE** FROM WHICH WE DEVELOP A POSITION.

WE CAME BACK FROM A WALK AND FOUND OUR FRONT DOOR STANDING **WIDE OPEN.**

MY PORRIDGE AND MY HUSBAND'S HAD CLEARLY BEEN TAMPERED WITH. YOU COULD EVEN SEE THE SPOON MARKS.

AND BABY BEAR'S HAD BEEN EATEN ALL UP.

IT WAS ALL GONE!!

HOW CAN A YOUNG BEAR GROW UP TO BE BIG AND STRONG WITHOUT ANY PORRIDGE?

HERE'S THE BEGINNING OF AN ARGUMENT BASED ON **EVIDENCE** --

-- THE BEARS ARE EXPLAINING:

❶ **WHAT** happened,

❷ **HOW** it happened,

❸ **WHO** was affected, and

❹ **WHY** it's a problem.

EMBEDDED IN ALL OF THOSE "QUESTION WORDS" IS A COMPLEX SET OF:

WHAT — Facts

HOW — Circumstances

WHO — Relationships

WHY — Reasons

...THESE CAN BE CRITICAL PARTS OF GOOD ARGUMENTS BASED ON EVIDENCE.

NOW -- WHAT IN THE **WORLD**?

POLICE

Y'KNOW, THEY WERE PROBABLY GOING TO HAVE A **CHEESE PLATE** OR SOMETHING IN THE JURY ROOM...

GIVE IT A **REST**, WILL YOU?

WHEN YOU TRY TO MAKE A PERSUASIVE ARGUMENT FOR COLLEGE OR FOR WORK, YOU MIGHT NOT USE THE KINDS OF CLAIMS AND EVIDENCE THAT A LAWYER WOULD CHOOSE.

YOU'LL NEED TO THINK ABOUT WHAT EVIDENCE WILL WORK IN THE CONTEXT OF **YOUR** ARGUMENT...

...AND HOW YOU CAN ORGANIZE AND PRESENT YOUR ARGUMENT MOST EFFECTIVELY.

IN CLASSROOMS AS IN COURTROOMS, ARGUMENTS ARE BUILT FROM THE GROUND UP --

EVIDENCE IS GATHERED, AND THEN LARGER CONCLUSIONS MAY BE DRAWN FROM IT.

SOMETIMES PRELIMINARY ARGUMENTS NEED TO BE REVISED...

CONCL-USIONS

EXTRAP-OLATION

EXAM-PLE   EXAM-PLE

ANALYSIS

EVIDENCE

BASE CLAIMS

GASP!

...AS...MORE EVIDENCE IS GATHERED...

FOCUSING ON EFFECTIVE ORGANIZATION

NOW WE'RE TALKING, LIZ!

ACADEMIC ARGUMENTS ARE MADE UP OF **PARAGRAPHS**. AND EVERY PARAGRAPH OF AN ARGUMENT NEEDS CERTAIN PARTS TO WORK AS A COHERENT UNIT.

IT'S LIKE THIS **SANDWICH**: YOU NEED MANY DIFFERENT COMPONENTS TO MAKE A PARAGRAPH **WHOLE**.

RIGHT -- EACH PARAGRAPH IS LIKE A MINI-ARGUMENT.

NO ONE WANTS AN ARGUMENT WITHOUT...

EVIDENCE --

SLICE!

ANALYSIS --

CHOP!

IMPLICATIONS --

DICE!

-- OR CONTEXT!

HALVE!

Issue 4 • Argument Beyond Pro and Con

The increasing generational differences between immigrants from Japan, the Issei, and the American-born second generation, the Nisei, had divided Japanese Americans even prior to the outbreak of World War II, and this division grew more apparent in the camps in which many Japanese Americans were interned during the war years. Nisei Gene Sogioka noted during his internment, "It's not just the age gap.... There are two different cultures in the camp: the Nisei, and the Issei" (qtd. in Gensensway 153). The disparity between ancient Japan and modernized America was embodied and displayed by the contrasting values, ideologies, and lifestyles of the Issei and Nisei. The Issei often insisted that Japanese be spoken throughout the camp; the Nisei, however, symbolized the idealistic quest for the "American Dream" and willingly conformed to U.S. customs (Dusselier 195). The camp structure intensified the estrangement between Issei parents and their Nisei children because the young people were no longer economically dependent on their parents; by taking away any rights to income or social status, the U.S. government had usurped the position of primary caregiver, and the structure of the Japanese American family unit neared disintegration (Ziegler 136; Dusselier 194). Due to the inability of each group to understand or accept the other's behaviors, an antagonistic relationship developed. Ted Matsuda, interned at Jerome, Arkansas, describes in his evacuation diary the frequent problems with stealing occurring in the camp (21). In his June 15 entry, he bitterly recounts, "Issei are quick to blame every fault on the Nisei" (21). Through the disunion between the Issei and Nisei, the cultural identification term "Japanese American" became fragmented by the opposing sides of its two competing ethnicities.

Adaptation of Marissa Osato essay, "Art in the Internment Camps: Designing the Japanese American Identity." Courtesy Marissa Osato.

SO-- --LET'S TALK ABOUT HOW THE PARTS OF AN ARGUMENT WORK AS A WHOLE.

B-BUT-- BUT MY SANDWICH--

WELCOME BACK!

YOU'RE JUST IN TIME FOR THE NEXT QUESTION!

PRO & CON

WHEN I WAS IN HIGH SCHOOL, THEY TAUGHT US TO WRITE FIVE-PARAGRAPH ESSAYS:

AN INTRODUCTION.

THREE EXAMPLES TO PROVE THE POINT.

AND A CONCLUSION THAT RESTATES THE INTRODUCTION.

WELL, MOST WRITING YOU DO AFTER HIGH SCHOOL WON'T FOLLOW SUCH A SIMPLE FORMULA.

RIGHT-- --PEOPLE DON'T USUALLY WRITE THAT WAY WHEN THEY HAVE SOMETHING TO SAY AND AN AUDIENCE TO SAY IT TO.

IN FACT, THE LAWS CREATED BY THE FAMILY EDUCATIONAL RIGHTS AND PRIVACY ACT [FERPA] REQUIRE THAT STUDENTS WAIVE IN WRITING THEIR RIGHT TO PRIVACY IF THEY'D LIKE THEIR PARENTS TO KNOW ABOUT THEIR GRADES.

CINDY'S GRADES

SO THE **LAW** IS ACTUALLY ON THE SIDE OF STUDENTS' PRIVACY.

WE CAN ARGUE WHETHER THAT LAW IS GOOD OR NOT.

IS IT USEFUL AND HELPFUL FOR STUDENTS' SUCCESS IN COLLEGE?

the LAW

WE COULD ALSO ASK ABOUT **CAUSE AND EFFECT** -- HOW MIGHT THE FERPA GUIDELINES LEAD TO GREATER STUDENT RESPONSIBILITY?

CAUSE & EFFECT

OR **NOT**?

ARGUING ALONG THESE LINES MIGHT ALSO ALLOW US TO ADDRESS THE QUESTION OF THE VALUES REPRESENTED BY THE GUIDELINES.

VALUES

FURTHERMORE, WHILE WE SEEM TO BE STARTING FROM DIFFERENT POSITIONS IN THIS ARGUMENT...

...WE SHOULD ALSO CONSIDER WHAT BOTH POSITIONS HAVE IN COMMON.

YES!

BOTH ASSERTIONS ARE FRAMED BY THE DESIRE TO HAVE STUDENTS **SUCCEED** IN COLLEGE!

THAT'S **RIGHT!**

THESE ARE JUST TWO DIFFERENT METHODS FOR ACHIEVING THE COMMON GOAL OF STUDENT SUCCESS: ALLOWING PARENTS TO MONITOR STUDENTS FREQUENTLY...

...OR ALLOWING STUDENTS THE FREEDOM TO BECOME RESPONSIBLE FOR THEIR OWN GRADES, WITHOUT PARENTS AND GUARDIANS CONSTANTLY WATCHING OVER THEM.

BUT WAIT--

IF WE ARGUE THAT PARENTS SHOULD KNOW STUDENTS' GRADES...

...ARE WE ASSUMING THAT PARENTS KNOW BEST HOW TO MOTIVATE THEIR CHILDREN TO DO BETTER?

INDEED!

REPORT CARD

— A
— B

WE MAY BE MAKING THAT ASSUMPTION IF WE RELEASE GRADE INFORMATION.

YOU MIGHT HAVE THE START OF A GOOD COUNTER-ARGUMENT.

HMPH.

PRECISELY.

I ARGUE THAT COLLEGE IS ONE OF THE FEW PLACES IN EARLY ADULTHOOD IN WHICH STUDENTS CAN MAKE MISTAKES --

-- SUCH AS DOING POORLY IN A CLASS --

-- AND THE CONSEQUENCES WILL NOT SEVERELY HAMPER THE STUDENT.

IT MAY RATHER SERVE AS A LEARNING OPPORTUNITY.

WAIT --

YOU'RE SAYING THAT YOU **WANT** STUDENTS TO **FAIL**?

NO, NO, NOT AT ALL.

I'M SAYING THAT FAILURE IN A COURSE --

-- WHILE AWFUL --

-- CAN BE A LEARNING EXPERIENCE.

THAT IS, **IF** THE STUDENT LEARNS FROM WHAT SHE OR HE DID WRONG IN THE FIRST PLACE.

UH, I'M IN COLLEGE MYSELF, AND MY MOTHER WOULD **KILL** ME IF I FAILED A CLASS.

FRAT

I'M SURE, YOUNG MAN.

JONATHAN AND LIZ, HOW WOULD YOU PREVENT SUCH A DRASTIC TURN OF EVENTS?

179

I DON'T HAVE MUCH OF A DRAFT YET FOR MY RESPONSE AND COUNTERARGUMENT ASSIGNMENT.

THAT'S OKAY.

YOU CAN COME TO OFFICE HOURS JUST TO HAVE A CONVERSATION ABOUT HOW TO GET STARTED.

SO...

...I READ THE BOOK BY ANYA KAMENETZ THAT YOU ASSIGNED, ABOUT REFORMING THE U.S. COLLEGE SYSTEM...

DIY U

ME TOO!

CAN WE TALK ABOUT IT TOGETHER?

SURE!

OKAY, SO...

...WHAT DID YOU THINK OF DIY U?

TO BE HONEST, MOSTLY I AGREE WITH THE AUTHOR.

I WORRY ABOUT THE RISING COST OF EDUCATION.

AND I WORRY ABOUT THE QUALITY OF EDUCATION I'M GETTING IN COLLEGE.

ch-CHING! ch-CHING!

$138 per class hour!!

$ $ $ $ $ $

ch-ch-ching

I USED TO THINK IT WAS ALL ABOUT GETTING GOOD GRADES, BUT NOW THAT TUITION FOR COLLEGE KEEPS GOING UP...

GRADES A

BILL $

ABSOLUTELY! STUDENTS ARE RIGHT TO WORRY ABOUT GETTING GOOD GRADES AND KEEPING THEIR PARENTS HAPPY.

BUT A LOT OF THEM ALSO CARE ABOUT THE BIG PICTURE AND THEIR FINANCIAL FUTURES.

KAMENETZ'S FIRST BOOK WAS CALLED **GENERATION DEBT**.

IT WAS ABOUT HOW YOUNG PEOPLE WERE OVERWHELMED BY STUDENT LOANS.

TO MAKE A FOCUSED RESPONSE TO **DIY U**, IT MIGHT BE GOOD TO PICK A PARTICULAR ARGUMENT KAMENETZ MAKES AND START THERE.

UH...

...SHE SPENDS A LOT OF HER BOOK TRYING TO EXPLAIN THE RISING COST OF TUITION.

I KEPT WANTING DIRECT REASONS FOR WHY TUITION IS GOING UP...

...BUT KAMENETZ SAYS THAT THE EXPLANATION MUST BE BASED ON A LOT OF DIFFERENT FACTORS --

-- AND WE DON'T KNOW ALL OF THEM.

IF MORE PEOPLE WANT TO GO TO COLLEGE, AND MORE COLLEGES ARE OFFERING THEIR SERVICES, SHOULDN'T IT GET CHEAPER BECAUSE OF THE COMPETITION?

U of YOU   QWIK-COLLEGE   McCollege   Unive ON A Stick

I WISH IT WERE THAT SIMPLE!

THINK OF WHAT WE TALKED ABOUT IN CLASS.

EXPLAINING RISING TUITION RATES IS LIKE EXPLAINING WHY STUDENTS' GRADES HAVE IMPROVED.

YOU NEED TO GRAPPLE WITH CONFLICTING THEORIES.

COLLEGE IS PART OF THE "AMERICAN DREAM," SO POTENTIAL STUDENTS CREATE A HUGE DEMAND FOR HIGHER EDUCATION.

HIGH DEMAND DRIVES UP PRICES, ESPECIALLY WHEN SO MANY STUDENTS WANT TO GO TO A SELECTIVE FOUR-YEAR SCHOOL.

THAT DEMAND IS STOKED BY MARKETERS WHO WANT TO ATTRACT STUDENTS BY "SELLING" THE IMAGE OF CERTAIN COLLEGES TO MAKE THEIR "BRANDS" ATTRACTIVE.

THAT DEMAND IS ALSO DRIVEN UP BY LOAN POLICIES THAT MAKE A LARGE AMOUNT OF CREDIT AVAILABLE TO YOUNG BORROWERS AS LONG AS THEY USE IT FOR COLLEGE.

KAMENETZ ALSO SAYS THAT SUPPLY AND DEMAND IS ONLY PART OF THE STORY.

IN ADDITION TO ECONOMIC FACTORS, LOTS OF OTHER FACTORS ARE INVOLVED IN HOW COLLEGES ARE PRICED.

PLUS, THERE ARE POLITICAL AND EMOTIONAL FACTORS THAT CAN BE HARD TO BOIL DOWN TO NUMBERS.

EMOTIONS
DUTY
STATUS
PRESTIGE
LEGACY

OKAY, BUT I'M NOT SURE I GOT THAT PART ABOUT COMPARING THE COST OF HIGHER EDUCATION TO THE COST OF HEALTH CARE...

WELL, LET'S TAKE A LOOK AT THAT PASSAGE.

COMING UP IN THE NEXT EXCITING EPISODE OF **REFRAME** ➤ "Get it **TOGETHER!**" [pg. 209]

WALK the TALK

"ARGUMENT"

WHETHER YOU'RE MAKING OR ANALYZING AN ARGUMENT, START WITH THE CLAIM. DOES IT GO BEYOND A SIMPLE PRO-AND-CON POSITION TO CONSIDER MORE THAN ONE VIEWPOINT?

LUIS'S FIRST DRAFT HAS A STRONG CLAIM TO MAKE. WHAT IS IT ARGUING FOR? DOES IT ADDRESS MULTIPLE PERSPECTIVES?

1 WHAT'S the CLAIM?

Text Memo • Luis • Last saved 3:14 pm

"The policy banning phones in class limits students' ability to compose. Today's students benefit from technologies that have enhanced their opportunities for reading, researching, and writing. Unfortunately many campuses are introducing strict rules against having phones visible in the classroom. Last week I used my phone to record an interview for an oral history project. It's an important writing tool for me. Plus looking up sources on my phone is a good way to contribute to class discussion. Phones encourage students to participate actively in coursework."

WHETHER YOU'RE EXAMINING YOUR OWN ARGUMENT OR SOMEONE ELSE'S, YOU CAN EVALUATE WHETHER AN ARGUMENT IS APPROPRIATE AND PERSUASIVE...

...BY EXAMINING ITS CLAIMS, THE SUPPORTING EVIDENCE, AND HOW CLEARLY AND EFFECTIVELY THE WRITER MAKES THE CASE.

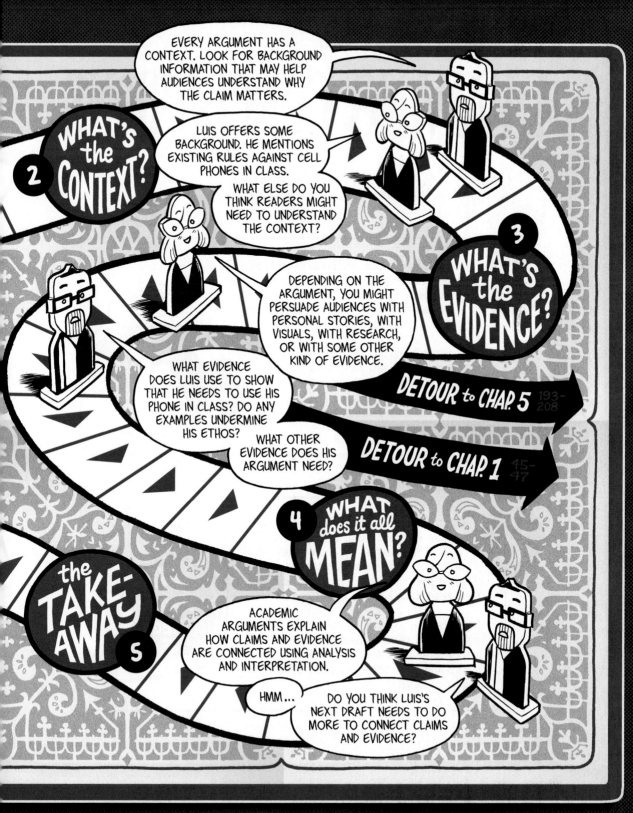

DRAWING CONCLUSIONS

The following assignments ask you to
think about creating effective arguments.

1 Map out the financial and personal costs of your
college education and the financial and personal
gains you hope to get from it. Use both text
and visuals to present compelling information
about your college costs.

What argument do you think your map
is making? Write a few paragraphs
explaining how you would persuade an
interested audience (such as a family
member) that your studies are -- or
are not -- worthwhile.

2 Choose an episode of a TV show you're very
familiar with, and try to think about the
kinds of "arguments" the show makes outside
of its plot. (Crime dramas often argue
against government bureaucracy as much as
they clearly take a stance against crime.)

Once you have some thoughts on the show's
arguments, think about how it goes about
making those arguments: is it purely through
storytelling, or do visuals and other elements
play a part as well?

3 Create your own short dramatic script using a popular fable or fairy tale, and imagine how characters might interact in a courtroom setting. Try performing the scenes in small groups for your classmates.

4 Create a plan for a Web site that would discuss an issue that interests you in an engaging way. How would you show the seriousness (or lack of seriousness) of the issue to a particular audience? What evidence would you need to include on the site, and how would you present that evidence -- using links? text? images? media files? How would you organize the site?

Present your plan to a small group of classmates and collect feedback on your site proposal.

MULTIPLYING YOUR RESEARCH OPTIONS

RHETORIC BUILDING

SO MUCH FOR THE **PROTEST**.

YEAH, WHAT'RE WE S'POSED TO DO WITH ALL OF THESE LEFTOVER SIGNS?

YIKES!

COYOTE!

~SLIP INSIDE!~

SO LET'S TAKE A CLOSER LOOK AT HOW TO **MANAGE** COLLABORATIVE PROBLEM-SOLVING, AS WELL AS THE KINDS OF COLLABORATIVE WRITING YOU MIGHT BE CALLED UPON TO DO ON CAMPUS.

UM, LIZ.

SPEAKING OF PROBLEMS...

eek!!

HEY!

I WAS SAVING THAT FOR THE NEXT CHAPTER!

SHOULD WE CALL ANIMAL CONTROL?

CALLING ANIMAL CONTROL DOESN'T ADDRESS THE BASIC PROBLEM. THIS COYOTE KEEPS COMING BACK. HE HAS A FONDNESS FOR PEANUT BUTTER SANDWICHES.

WE NEED TO FIGURE OUT HOW TO ADDRESS THIS WILD SITUATION.

THERE ARE COYOTES ALL OVER CAMPUS THESE DAYS.

WE COULD ORGANIZE A PROTEST MARCH AND STORM THE GATES OF THE ADMINISTRATION BUILDING!

Yeah!

AND IF THAT DOESN'T WORK WE CAN TAKE THE LAW INTO OUR OWN HANDS!

Right on!

UM, EXCUSE ME...

EXCUSE ME!

OH, HEY, FLORA.

STILL ROCKIN' THE **PITH HELMET**, I SEE.

LOOK, PROTESTS AND MOBS ARE...UH, **OPTIONS**...

BUT LET'S SEE IF WE CAN COME UP WITH A BETTER PLAN.

WHITE-BOARD STORAGE CLOSET

IF WE REALLY WANT TO KEEP THESE COYOTES OFF CAMPUS...

...LET'S BEGIN BY CONSIDERING THE **CONTEXT** OF THIS SITUATION.

LITTLE HELP?

CONTEXT? WELL, LET'S SEE. I DON'T THINK COYOTES ARE **ENDANGERED** OR ANYTHING.

NO, BUT MANY COYOTES ARE ADAPTING TO SUBURBAN AND URBAN HABITATS AS DEVELOP-MENT SPREADS.

WE'VE BEEN STUDYING THIS IN MY ZOOLOGY CLASS.

HEY, THIS PLACEMAT TURNED OUT GREAT!

YEAH, BUT YOU KNOW...

COYOTES ON CAMPUS
HOW WE CAN **ALL** HELP:

...WE'VE BEEN FOCUSING ON REACHING **STUDENTS**. BUT MAYBE THERE ARE **OTHERS** WHOSE HELP WE NEED TO SOLVE THIS PROBLEM.

LIKE INSTRUCTORS? AND STAFF?

RIGHT!

ADMINISTRATORS
STAFF
STUDENTS
INSTRUCTORS

AUDIENCE

YOU KNOW, OUR **CAMPUS ADMINISTRATION** NEEDS TO TAKE ACTION, TOO.

WE COULD ADDRESS THE COYOTE PROBLEM IN A PRESENTATION EXPLAINING HOW THE ADMINISTRATION CAN GET INVOLVED.

I THINK I EVEN KNOW WHAT **HOOK** TO USE!

IMAGINE A MAN. A MAN WHO LOST HIS LUNCH...TO A **COYOTE**!

gasp!

SO NOW WE'RE TACKLING THE COYOTE ISSUE ON **TWO** FRONTS!

PLACEMAT
1
AUTHOR   STUDENTS

PRESENTATION
2
AUTHOR   ADMINISTRATION

YOUR TWO TEXTS MAY BE VERY DIFFERENT BECAUSE YOU ARE APPEALING TO DIFFERENT AUDIENCES.

BUT STUDENTS AND ADMINISTRATORS WILL NEED TO WORK TOGETHER TO GET THE PROBLEM SOLVED.

SOMETIMES COLLABORATION INVOLVES COORDINATING MULTIPLE **SMALLER** PROJECTS TO SOLVE A **LARGER** PROBLEM.

MANAGING COLLABORATIVE WRITING PROJECTS

YOU'VE **THOUGHT** COLLABORATIVELY ABOUT YOUR GOALS, BUT YOU ALSO NEED TO **WORK** COLLABORATIVELY TO ACCOMPLISH THEM.

TEXT

AUTHORS

AUDIENCE

YOU'LL NEED TO DIVIDE UP THE DUTIES FAIRLY...

...AND EVEN WITH MULTIPLE AUTHORS YOU'LL WANT TO MAINTAIN CONSISTENCY IN YOUR MESSAGE.

TEN MINUTES LATER...

WHAT'S WRONG?

BICKER BICKER

LUIS WANTS TO MAKE THE CONTENT APPROACHABLE BY USING PERSONAL STORIES, BUT FLORA WANTS TO EMPHASIZE SCIENTIFIC RESEARCH AND FACTS.

ADMINISTRATORS ARE PERHAPS LESS LIKELY TO BE PERSUADED BY PERSONAL STORIES. THERE ARE MANY POINTS OF VIEW ON EVERY ISSUE.

A PERSONAL STORY CAN WORK WELL AS A HOOK TO GET YOUR AUDIENCE INTERESTED. BUT YOU'LL WANT DATA, TOO, TO DEMONSTRATE THAT THE PROBLEM IS WIDESPREAD AND SERIOUS.

ADMINISTRATORS

PERSONAL ANEC-DOTE

DATA

REFRAME
with
Luis & Cindy

Get it TOGETHER!

HEY, GUYS, CAN WE GET TOGETHER TODAY? I NEED YOUR HELP.

AND SO...

HI, FLORA, WHAT'S UP?

CAMPUS COFFEE

HEY! LIZ ASKED US TO GET PEER FEEDBACK ON SUMMARIES OF AN ARTICLE WE HAD TO READ.

WHAT'S THE SUMMARY ABOUT?

IT'S ACTUALLY ABOUT **TEXTING.**

IT'S AN ARTICLE WITH THREE COAUTHORS. THEY PUBLISHED THEIR RESEARCH IN A JOURNAL CALLED *THE HEALTH EDUCATOR.*

SCHOLARLY RESEARCH ABOUT TEXTING? SOUNDS INTERESTING!

DOESN'T THAT SOUND INTERESTING, CINDY?

bleep-BLOOP!

...HMM?

HERE'S MY SUMMARY.

Hudson, Bliss, and Fetro talked to four groups of students to figure out how text messaging shapes how college students think about personal health. Text messaging is often linked to negative consequences such as sleep deprivation, lousy driving, and random hook-ups.But the authors wanted to gather information directly from college students rather than rely on sterotypes about kids today. The students in the four groups talked a lot about "comfort," "control," and "dependancy."When asked if they thought text messaging had a more positive or negative impact on their health, the results were confusing. They said texting allowed them to keep in touch, flirt with less awkwardness, and get better jobs, but it definitely led to more jealousy in their love lives.

COMING UP IN THE NEXT EXCITING EPISODE OF **REFRAME**

"Wrong turns or shortcuts?"

[pg. 245]

DRAWING CONCLUSIONS

The following assignments ask you to practice finding,
evaluating, and responding to research sources.

1 Make an inventory of all your past experiences
with collaboration. Think broadly about when,
where, and how you have worked with other
people on any kind of project.

List all the ways in which your collective efforts
resulted in a better outcome than individual work
might have provided. What challenges did you face?
How did you resolve them? Write a short personal
guide for your peers about working collaboratively.

2 Throughout this book the characters
interact with different social media
platforms. How are such platforms
collaborative forms of knowledge building
and sharing?

In interacting socially on such platforms, have
you developed insights and ideas that you
otherwise might not have had?

Compose a blog post in which you consider
how such platforms are collaborative spaces,
and invite others to respond to your ideas.

3

Issues that could use some collaborative thinking and collective effort are all around us. Consider an issue facing your campus or neighborhood.

Begin brainstorming about the issue, and then reflect on how collaborating with others might work to address it.

Who should be involved? What kinds of thinking will you have to do together to understand and work on the issue? What kinds of tasks can be divvied up? What composing tools (e.g., collaborative authoring software) might assist your group in getting it together?

4

Cut out a rhetorical triangle to help you visualize at least two possible solutions for a specific problem on your campus.

Use one side for one approach and the flip side for the other. What media would work best to get your message out to the public?

Who is your audience, and what would motivate them to collaborate on the solution? Whom do you envision helping you on your composing team?

ISSUE **6**

RESEARCH:
MORE THAN DETECTIVE WORK

In this issue...

Issue 6 • Research: More Than Detective Work

TRACKING DOWN SOURCES

RESEARCHERS TODAY CAN ACCESS FAR MORE BOOKS, ARTICLES, DOCUMENTS, REPORTS, MULTIMEDIA, AND VISUAL RESOURCES THAN SCHOLARS OF THE PAST.

EVEN WHEN YOU'RE WORKING WITH A LOT OF SOURCES, YOU'RE LOOKING FOR THE BEST SOURCES POSSIBLE.

SEEK OUT BOTH QUANTITY AND QUALITY.

WITH SO MUCH INFORMATION OUT THERE, YOU NEED TO DO **DETECTIVE WORK** TO FIGURE OUT WHICH SOURCES TO USE.

DON'T MAKE THE MISTAKE OF RUSHING THROUGH THE PROCESS OF FINDING SOURCES.

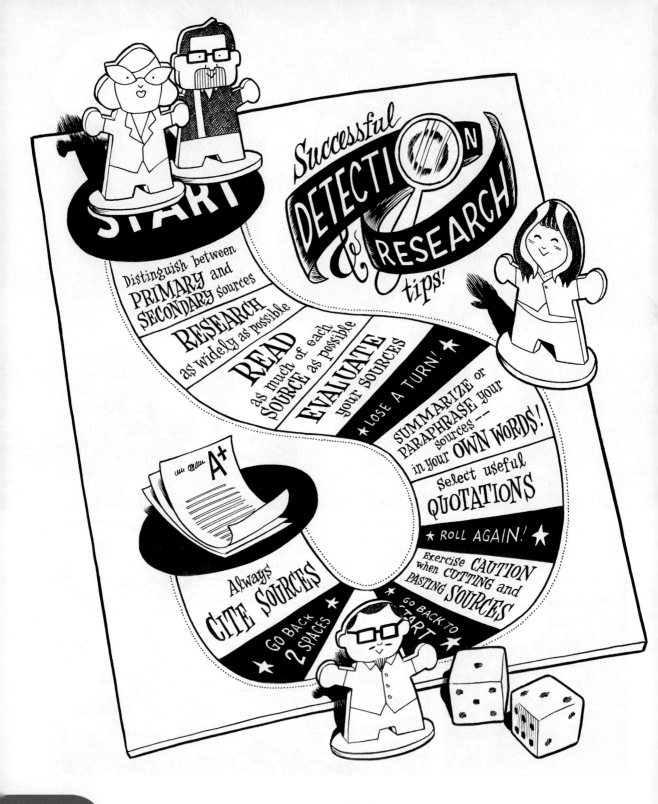

Issue 6 • Research: More Than Detective Work

BUT IF YOU WRITE A TELL-ALL BOOK YEARS LATER, THAT WON'T BE A PRIMARY SOURCE ANYMORE.

RIGHT?

ACTUALLY, IF I WITNESSED OR PARTICIPATED IN AN EVENT, HISTORIANS WOULD CONSIDER MY ACCOUNT A **PRIMARY SOURCE**...

...NO MATTER WHEN THE ACCOUNT WAS WRITTEN.

EXPERIMENTAL RESULTS AND FIELD RESEARCH ARE ALSO PRIMARY SOURCES THAT OTHER RESEARCHERS CAN BUILD ON.

GOVERNMENT DOCUMENTS CAN BE IMPORTANT PRIMARY SOURCES FOR RESEARCH PROJECTS AS WELL.

A PRIMARY SOURCE DOESN'T NEED TO BE A WRITTEN TEXT, EITHER.

PAINTINGS, SOUND RECORDINGS, FILMS, BUILDINGS -- ALL OF THESE AND MORE CAN BE PRIMARY SOURCES YOU MIGHT EXPLORE IN A CLASS OR IN OTHER WRITING CONTEXTS.

A **SECONDARY SOURCE** IS A SOURCE THAT DESCRIBES, ANALYZES, OR INTERPRETS A PRIMARY SOURCE.

BOOKS AND ARTICLES ABOUT LITERATURE, SCIENCE, OR ART MIGHT BE CONSIDERED SECONDARY SOURCES.

SO IF I WROTE AN ESSAY ABOUT ARTHUR MILLER'S *THE CRUCIBLE*, WHICH WAS ABOUT THE SALEM WITCH TRIALS IN MASSACHUSETTS IN 1692...

...AND USED A SCHOLARLY ARTICLE FROM A JOURNAL OF THEATER STUDIES...

...MILLER'S PLAY WOULD BE A **PRIMARY SOURCE**, AND THE JOURNAL ARTICLE WOULD BE A **SECONDARY SOURCE**.

RIGHT! THE ARTICLE PROVIDES AN INTERPRETATION OF MILLER'S PLAY.

WHAT'S TRICKY IS THAT A SECONDARY SOURCE IN ONE SITUATION MIGHT BE A PRIMARY SOURCE IN ANOTHER.

FOR EXAMPLE, THE SAME ARTICLE YOU'RE USING AS A SECONDARY SOURCE FOR YOUR PROJECT ON *THE CRUCIBLE* COULD BE A **PRIMARY SOURCE** FOR A RESEARCH PROJECT ON THE AUTHOR OF THE ARTICLE.

A SUBJECT LIKE THE SALEM WITCH TRIALS CAN INTEREST RESEARCHERS IN MANY FIELDS.

INDEED, SCHOLARS LOOK FOR DIFFERENT KINDS OF EVIDENCE IN APPROACHING THE SAME SUBJECT...

...AND THEY MAY EVEN DRAW DIFFERENT CONCLUSIONS FROM THE SAME EVIDENCE.

Bettmann/Getty Images

HISTORIANS WHO STUDY RACE LOOK AT HOW PERCEIVED RACIAL DIFFERENCES AND STEREOTYPES ABOUT SLAVES MIGHT HAVE PLAYED INTO THE PURITANS' HYSTERIA ABOUT WITCHES.

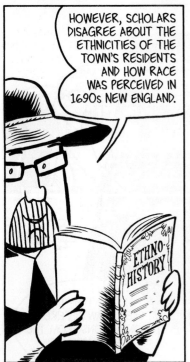

HOWEVER, SCHOLARS DISAGREE ABOUT THE ETHNICITIES OF THE TOWN'S RESIDENTS AND HOW RACE WAS PERCEIVED IN 1690s NEW ENGLAND.

ETHNO-HISTORY

ECONOMISTS MIGHT LOOK AT SUPPLY AND DEMAND TO UNDERSTAND THE EVENTS THAT TOOK PLACE IN SALEM VILLAGE, PARTICULARLY WHEN CROPS FAILED OR VILLAGERS SQUABBLED OVER PROPERTY RIGHTS.

SOMETIMES EVEN THE "FACTS" OF HISTORICAL CASES MAY BE OPEN TO DEBATE.

RAINFALL STATISTICS AND THE LOCATIONS OF PROPERTY LINES WEREN'T RECORDED AS CAREFULLY IN 1692 AS THEY ARE TODAY.

JOURNAL of ECONOMIC PERSPECTIVE

SOME SCHOLARS HAVE ARGUED THAT THE AFFLICTED PEOPLE OF SALEM WERE ACTUALLY HALLUCINATING AFTER EATING CONTAMINATED RYE.

RYE BREAD

YOU SHOULD CONSULT MULTIPLE SOURCES TO GET A SENSE OF THE SCHOLARLY DEBATES SURROUNDING YOUR RESEARCH TOPIC. NOT EVERYONE AGREES THAT WHAT THE PURITANS ATE WAS TO BLAME FOR THE SALEM WITCH HYSTERIA.

JOURNAL of RYE

RQ RYE QUARTERLY

STUDY: Rye Best for Grilled Cheese

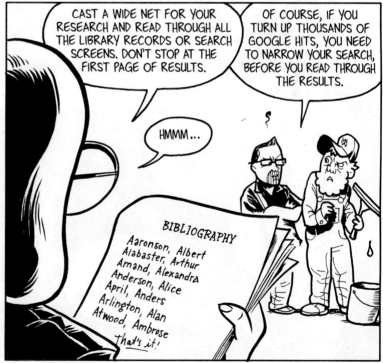

CAST A WIDE NET FOR YOUR RESEARCH AND READ THROUGH ALL THE LIBRARY RECORDS OR SEARCH SCREENS. DON'T STOP AT THE FIRST PAGE OF RESULTS.

OF COURSE, IF YOU TURN UP THOUSANDS OF GOOGLE HITS, YOU NEED TO NARROW YOUR SEARCH, BEFORE YOU READ THROUGH THE RESULTS.

HMMM...

BIBLIOGRAPHY
Aaronson, Albert
Alabaster, Arthur
Amand, Alexandra
Anderson, Alice
April, Anders
Arlington, Alan
Atwood, Ambrose
That's it!

Jonathan Alexander says:
HOWEVER, THERE ARE SOME SITUATIONS WHERE ONLINE SOURCES WITH A STRONG SELF-INTEREST, SUCH AS TWEETS AND STATUS UPDATES, MAY GIVE AN INSIDER'S VIEW OF CURRENT EVENTS.

@Lizlosh
THINK ABOUT WHICH SOURCES WILL BEST SERVE YOUR PURPOSE IN THIS CONTEXT.

89/160 Remaining

YOU CAN ALSO LOOK FOR INFORMATION ABOUT THE CREATOR OF A POTENTIAL SOURCE.

IS THIS PERSON A SCHOLAR, AN EXPERT, OR AN INFORMED OBSERVER? HOW CAN YOU FIND OUT?

IF THE PERSON TEACHES AT A UNIVERSITY, YOU MIGHT LOOK AT HIS OR HER FACULTY WEB PAGE.

Alexander, Jonathan

Professor of English and Director of the Center for Excellence in Writing and Communication at the University of California, Irvine.

IT MIGHT GIVE YOU A BETTER SENSE OF THE SCHOLAR'S PERSONALITY, RESEARCH INTERESTS, AND DEPTH OF KNOWLEDGE ON THE SUBJECT.

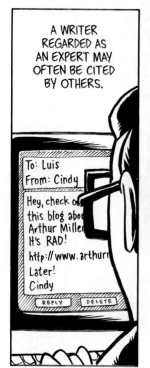

A WRITER REGARDED AS AN EXPERT MAY OFTEN BE CITED BY OTHERS.

To: Luis
From: Cindy

Hey, check o~
this blog abou~
Arthur Mille~
H's RAD!
http://www.arthur~
Later!
Cindy

REPLY   DELETE

Reference + Information

A LIBRARY'S CATALOG AND DATABASES CAN SHOW THE ACADEMIC WORK THAT A PARTICULAR AUTHOR HAS PUBLISHED.

YOU CAN USE AN INTERNET SEARCH ENGINE TO FIND OUT ABOUT WRITERS WHO AREN'T ACADEMICS.

MANY AUTHORS HAVE PERSONAL WEB PAGES WITH INFORMATION ABOUT THEIR WORK.

CHECK A SOURCE'S DATE OF PUBLICATION.

A RECENT BOOK OR ARTICLE IS LIKELY TO CONTAIN REFERENCES TO THE MOST CURRENT RESEARCH.

DISCIPLINES SUCH AS THE SCIENCES MAY REQUIRE UP-TO-DATE SOURCES, SINCE KNOWLEDGE IN THOSE DISCIPLINES CHANGES RAPIDLY.

the BENEFITS of LEECHES 1756

IN OTHER DISCIPLINES, SUCH AS HISTORY, OLDER ACCOUNTS MIGHT SOMETIMES BE APPROPRIATE.

A WORD OF CAUTION: THINK CAREFULLY ABOUT POPULAR PERIODICALS.

IF YOUR BEST SOURCE IS A NEWSPAPER ARTICLE, YOU SHOULD PROBABLY KEEP LOOKING.

POPULAR NEWS
She Sings!

JOURNALISTS OFTEN HAVE GOOD GENERAL KNOWLEDGE...

...AND GOOD WRITING SKILLS...

BUT MOST REPORTERS AREN'T SPECIALISTS WITH IN-DEPTH KNOWLEDGE OF THE TOPIC.

INSTEAD, SEE IF THE NEWSPAPER ARTICLE MENTIONS A PROFESSOR, A GOVERNMENT OFFICIAL, OR ANOTHER EXPERT ON THE TOPIC, AND THEN SEARCH FOR INFORMATION FROM THESE SPECIFIC SOURCES.

ADS

MAKING SOURCES TALK: SUMMARY, PARAPHRASE, QUOTATION

SUMMARY

SETTING UP CONTEXTS AND PROVIDING BACKGROUND INFORMATION

PARAPHRASE

GIVING A SENSE OF THE AUTHOR'S ARGUMENT

QUOTATION

DRAWING ATTENTION TO SOMETHING PARTICULARLY EVOCATIVE OR INSIGHTFUL IN THE AUTHOR'S OWN WORDS

LET'S TALK ABOUT SUMMARIZING, PARAPHRASING, AND QUOTING -- HOW TO DO THEM, WHEN, AND WHY.

SUMMARIZING

PRESENTS A CONCISE, GENERAL SENSE OF WHAT YOUR SOURCE IS ABOUT.

OFTEN, SUMMARIZING GIVES A BROAD OVERVIEW OF MATERIAL THAT IS NOT IN DISPUTE.

HERE'S A SUMMARY THAT USES CONTENT FROM A WIKIPEDIA ARTICLE:

"The history of detective fiction dates back to 1841, when Edgar Allan Poe introduced Monsieur C. Auguste Dupin in the short story 'The Murders in the Rue Morgue.' Today it includes the police procedural, the legal thriller, the courtroom drama, the locked room mystery, hard-boiled fiction, the noir novel, and the 'cozy,' in which sex and violence are downplayed. In the 'cozy,' the protagonist is often a female amateur, and humor and social satire might be important parts of the narrative."

BRRT!!

I HOPE YOU PLAN TO **CITE** THAT SOURCE, SINCE YOU ARE USING SOME VERY **SPECIALIZED** KNOWLEDGE.

ABSOLUTELY.

EVEN WHEN THE WORDS ARE MINE, I HAVE TO CITE SOURCES WHEN I USE THE IDEAS OF OTHERS.

WHEN I'M SUMMARIZING MY SOURCES, I ALWAYS RECORD INFORMATION ABOUT EACH SOURCE SO I KNOW EXACTLY WHERE I FOUND IT.

BRRRT!

WOULD YOU **STOP** THAT?

SINCE WIKIPEDIA IS COLLABORATIVELY AUTHORED AND FREQUENTLY CHANGED, NOT EVERYONE CONSIDERS IT A RELIABLE SOURCE.

YES.

BUT LUCKILY, GOOD WIKIPEDIA ARTICLES OFTEN CITE AUTHORITATIVE SOURCES, SO YOU CAN CONTINUE YOUR DETECTIVE WORK THERE.

SO, IN **SUMMARY**...

=WINK=

...SUMMARIES MAY JUST RESTATE INFORMATION THE READER ALREADY KNOWS, LIKE THE GENERAL PLOT OF A NOVEL OR THE MAIN IDEAS OF A NONFICTION TEXT...

...BUT SUMMARIES CAN ALSO PROVIDE INFORMATION THAT IS NEW, INTERESTING, AND RELEVANT.

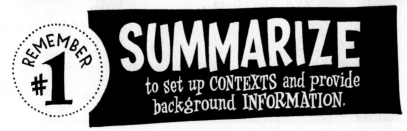

REMEMBER #1

SUMMARIZE
to set up CONTEXTS and provide background INFORMATION.

PARAPHRASING

SHOULD GIVE THE READER A MORE COMPLETE SENSE OF THE AUTHOR'S ARGUMENT AND MORE OF THE FLAVOR OF THE ORIGINAL THAN A SUMMARY.

AND EVEN THOUGH A PARAPHRASE IS "IN YOUR OWN WORDS," THE IDEAS CAME FROM SOMEWHERE ELSE -- SO YOU'LL HAVE TO CITE YOUR SOURCE.

HERE'S A PARAPHRASE OF PART OF A CHAPTER IN THE BOOK *CITY OF QUARTZ*, A HISTORY OF LOS ANGELES.

AUTHOR MIKE DAVIS CLAIMS THAT NOIR STORIES ABOUT CRIME AND THE ILL EFFECTS OF CAPITALISM REFLECT MANY DIFFERENT INFLUENCES FROM THE TIME OF THE GREAT DEPRESSION, WORLD WAR II, AND THE PERIOD THAT FOLLOWED.

DAVIS ARGUES THAT IMMIGRANT WRITERS, COMPOSERS, FILMMAKERS, AND ARTISTS FLEEING HITLER'S GERMANY PLAYED A ROLE IN DEVELOPING CERTAIN ASPECTS OF THE NOIR DETECTIVE GENRE, BUT HE INSISTS THAT FEW OF THEM ACTUALLY PARTICIPATED IN THE GRITTY URBAN LIFESTYLES OF LOS ANGELES IN THE 1940s.

UNLIKE MANY CRITICS, DAVIS ASSERTS THAT LOCAL LOS ANGELES AUTHORS PLAYED A MAJOR ROLE IN DEVELOPING WHAT CAME TO BE KNOWN AS "L.A. NOIR."

HE SAYS THAT THESE LOCAL WRITERS KNEW MUCH MORE ABOUT THE SCANDALS OF THE CITY -- POLICE CORRUPTION, REAL ESTATE AND OIL SPECULATION, AND ANTI-LABOR AND ANTI-IMMIGRANT POLITICS -- THAN OUTSIDERS COMING FROM EUROPE DID.

WOW!

THAT PARAPHRASE REALLY GAVE ME A SENSE OF DAVIS'S ARGUMENT AND OF WHY HIS SCHOLARSHIP IS DISTINCTIVE.

← PARAPHRASE   SUMMARY →

SO, WHEN YOU FIND A SOURCE THAT IS REALLY SIGNIFICANT FOR YOUR RESEARCH, EVEN IF YOU DISAGREE WITH IT, YOU MIGHT WANT TO SPEND SOME TIME CAREFULLY PARAPHRASING IT IN YOUR OWN WORDS.

REMEMBER #2

PARAPHRASE
to give a sense of the author's ARGUMENT.

NOW, **QUOTING** COMES IN HANDY WHEN YOUR SOURCES SAY SOMETHING PARTICULARLY **EVOCATIVE**...

...OR **INSIGHTFUL**...

...OR WHEN YOU WANT TO CALL ATTENTION TO A WRITER'S **LANGUAGE**.

YOU CAN QUOTE A SHORT PASSAGE OR EVEN JUST A SIGNIFICANT KEYWORD.

GENIUS!

IF YOU CHOOSE TO PRESENT A LONG QUOTATION, MAKE SURE THAT YOU HAVE ENOUGH TO SAY ABOUT THE PASSAGE TO SHOW WHY IT'S WORTH REPRODUCING IN ITS ENTIRETY.

FOR INSTANCE...

LAUGHING in the JUNGLE
LOUIS ADAMIC

LAUGHING IN THE JUNGLE, A BOOK ABOUT LOS ANGELES BY IMMIGRANT WRITER LOUIS ADAMIC, HAS A DISTINCTIVE WRITING STYLE AND MANY JUICY PASSAGES TO CHOOSE FROM.

HERE ARE ADAMIC'S PROVOCATIVE INSIGHTS ON THE CITY:

"FROM MOUNT HOLLYWOOD, LOS ANGELES LOOKS RATHER NICE. ..."

"ACTUALLY, AND IN SPITE OF ALL THE HEALTHFUL SUNSHINE AND OCEAN BREEZES, IT IS A **BAD** PLACE, FULL OF OLD, DYING PEOPLE, AND YOUNG PEOPLE WHO WERE BORN OLD OF TIRED PIONEER PARENTS, VICTIMS OF AMERICA --

" --FULL OF CURIOUS WILD AND POISONOUS GROWTHS, DECADENT RELIGIONS AND CULTS AND FAKE SCIENCE, AND WILDCAT BUSINESS ENTERPRISES, WHICH, WITH THEIR AIM FOR QUICK PROFITS, ARE DOOMED TO COLLAPSE AND DRAG DOWN MULTITUDES OF PEOPLE...

"...A JUNGLE."

IF YOU DON'T NEED THE WHOLE QUOTATION, YOU CAN WEAVE SHORT QUOTED DESCRIPTIONS INTO YOUR OWN PROSE.

NOTICE THAT, IN EACH CASE, WE USE QUOTATION MARKS, PROVIDE AN IN-TEXT CITATION (THIS ONE FOLLOWS MLA STYLE), AND EMPHASIZE OUR OWN COMMENTARY.

"Adamic gives us verbal images that contradict a popular picture of health. Terms such as 'poisonous,' 'dying,' and 'decadent' (220) provide a stark contrast with the 'sunshine and ocean breezes' typically associated with L.A."

tap tap

REMEMBER #3

QUOTE to draw attention to the author's own WORDS and PHRASING.

241

AND THIS IS PRETTY MUCH HOW WE WANT LIZ AND JONATHAN TO LOOK, AND THESE CHARACTERS WERE JUST THERE FOR THE **TAKING** ON THE INTERNET...

...SO WE FIGURED IT WOULD BE OKAY.

UM, GUYS...

...EVEN MATERIAL YOU FIND ONLINE WAS CREATED BY SOMEBODY.*

RIGHT! SOMEBODY WHO DESERVES CREDIT FOR THE WORK.

OKAY.

*In this case, Tom Gammill, creator of The Doozies.

IS THIS BETTER?

I-IT'S **BETTER**, RIGHT?

NO!

AND WHAT ABOUT YOUR CREDIBILITY AS AN ARTIST? YOU DON'T WANT PEOPLE TO THINK YOU DON'T HAVE A STYLE OF YOUR OWN...

...AND SOMETHING OF YOUR OWN TO SAY.

YOU SHOULD **TALK** TO US IF YOU'RE HAVING TROUBLE HANDLING A PROJECT.

PRESENTING OTHERS' WORK AS YOUR OWN IS A TERRIBLE IDEA FOR A LOT OF REASONS.

FOR ONE THING, IT'S **PLAGIARISM**.

BUT JUST A COUPLE OF PAGES BACK YOU GUYS WERE TALKING ABOUT QUOTING FROM SOURCES.

BUT YOU NEED TO TELL READERS WHERE YOU FOUND YOUR SOURCES, NOT PRETEND YOU CREATED THE WORK YOURSELF.

AND YOU ALSO NEED TO EVALUATE AND INTERPRET MATERIAL THAT YOU FIND AND INTEGRATE IT INTO YOUR OWN TEXT.

YOU DON'T JUST INSERT SOURCES WITHOUT ANY ANALYSIS OR REFLECTION!

IF YOU ARE GOING TO QUOTE SOMEONE ELSE'S WORK, HAVE A GOOD REASON FOR REPRODUCING IT EXACTLY.

SIGH

THAT MAKES SENSE.

I GUESS WE KNEW ALL THAT, BUT DESPERATION MAKES PEOPLE DO CRAZY THINGS SOMETIMES.

IT'S NOT ALWAYS EASY TO CITE YOUR SOURCES.

OUR STUDENTS HAVE TROUBLE WITH IT ALL THE TIME.

HOW DO I CITE A VIDEO I WATCHED **ONLINE**?

WHAT ABOUT A **COMIC**?

Issue 6 • Research: More Than Detective Work

REFRAME with Luis & Cindy

Wrong turns or shortcuts?

I HOPE COMING TO THE LIBRARY WASN'T A WASTE OF TIME.

SEARCHING ON GOOGLE MIGHT WORK JUST AS WELL.

DEPENDS ON THE SUBJECT, I GUESS.

WHAT ARE YOU WORKING ON?

A PROJECT ON FRACKING.

IT'S A TECHNIQUE FOR EXTRACTING NATURAL GAS FROM ROCK.

I KNOW. THEY USE HIGH-PRESSURE FLUIDS.

IT'S CONTROVERSIAL BECAUSE SOME PEOPLE ARE CONCERNED ABOUT ENVIRONMENTAL CONSEQUENCES.

WHAT ABOUT THIS?

"DOES FRACKING ROCK OR DOES FRACKING SHAKE US UP?"

IT'S THE FIRST RESULT.

FRACK ATTACK!

play the GAME!

COOL WEB SITE. IT MAKES A **STRONG ARGUMENT** USING ANIMATION.

YEAH, THEY EVEN HAVE A VIDEO GAME THAT SHOWS HOW GEOLOGICAL FORCES INTERACT.

BUT THE WEB SITE DOESN'T CITE THE SOURCES FOR ALL THE STATISTICS THEY LIST.

I CAN'T FIGURE OUT WHO **SPONSORS** THE SITE.

OH, HERE IT IS! "COURTESY OF **FRACK ATTACK**, THE MOVIE."

THIS RESEARCH DOESN'T SEEM ALL THAT **OBJECTIVE**. PARTICULARLY IF IT'S PROMOTING A FILM.

THIS VIDEO GAME IS **INTRIGUING**, THOUGH.

MAYBE I SHOULD **PLAY** A LITTLE BIT...JUST TO SEE IF IT'S, YOU KNOW, **EDUCATIONAL**.

CAN I HELP?

WHAT'S YOUR TOPIC?

I'M DOING RESEARCH ON FRACKING.

I NEED TO FIND SCHOLARLY SOURCES.

YOU MIGHT WANT TO START WITH THE SCHOLARLY DATABASE **JSTOR**.

IT HAS ARTICLES FROM **MANY** SUBJECT AREAS, INCLUDING SCIENCE, LAW, HISTORY, SOCIOLOGY, PSYCHOLOGY, LITERATURE...

TRY TYPING IN YOUR SEARCH TERMS.

JSTOR

SEARCH

JSTOR

fracking

SEARCH

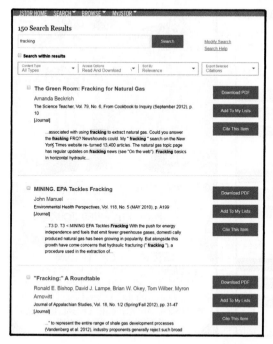

JSTOR HOME   SEARCH ▾   BROWSE ▾   MYJSTOR ▾

150 Search Results

fracking   Search   Modify Search
                                                  Search Help

☐ Search within results

| Content Type | Access Options | Sort By | Export Selected |
| All Types | Read And Download | Relevance | Citations |

☐ The Green Room: Fracking for Natural Gas
Amanda Beckrich
The Science Teacher, Vol. 79, No. 6, From Cookbook to Inquiry (September 2012), p. 10
[Journal]

...associated with using **fracking** to extract natural gas. Could you answer the **fracking** FRQ? Newshounds could. My " **fracking** " search on the New York Times website re- turned 13,400 articles. The natural gas topic page has regular updates on **fracking** news (see "On the web"). **Fracking** basics in horizontal hydraulic...

Download PDF
Add To My Lists
Cite This Item

☐ MINING. EPA Tackles Fracking
John Manuel
Environmental Health Perspectives, Vol. 118, No. 5 (MAY 2010), p. A199
[Journal]

...T3 D. T3 < MINING EPA Tackles **Fracking** With the push for energy independence and fuels that emit fewer greenhouse gases, domesti cally produced natural gas has been growing in popularity. But alongside this growth have come concerns that hydraulic fracturing (" **fracking** "), a procedure used in the extraction of...

Download PDF
Add To My Lists
Cite This Item

☐ "Fracking:" A Roundtable
Ronald E. Bishop, David J. Lampe, Brian W. Okey, Tom Wilber, Myron Arnowitt
Journal of Appalachian Studies, Vol. 18, No. 1/2 (Spring/Fall 2012), pp. 31-47
[Journal]

...' to represent the entire range of shale gas development processes (Vandenberg et al 2012). industry proponents generally reject such broad

Download PDF
Add To My Lists
Cite This Item

OH NO, THESE RESULTS ARE ALL OVER THE MAP!

THERE ARE ARTICLES FROM ENVIRONMENTAL HEALTH PERSPECTIVES, BUT ALSO THE SCIENCE TEACHER, JOURNAL OF APPALACHIAN STUDIES, MATHEMATICS TEACHING IN THE MIDDLE SCHOOL, AND SOCIALIST LAWYER!

I'M NOT SURE WHAT ALL OF THESE HAVE TO DO WITH FRACKING!

AND *SOCIALIST LAWYER* SOUNDS LIKE A JOURNAL WITH A POLITICAL AGENDA. IT DOESN'T SEEM LIKE AN OBJECTIVE SOURCE.

LET'S TRY THIS...

LET'S TRY A SEARCH USING PRECISE TECHNICAL TERMS.

WHAT SHOULD I ENTER?

HMM...

CINDY, WHAT DO YOU THINK WOULD BE A GOOD --

CINDY?

click click

COME ON...

WOOT!

I TOOK OUT THE **HYDRAULIC FRACKER**!

BING! BING!

UH, HOW ABOUT "HYDRAULIC FRACTURING" RATHER THAN "FRACKING"?

GOOD IDEA. SOMETIMES QUOTATION MARKS IMPROVE RESULTS.

THEY LIMIT RESULTS TO THE SPECIFIC PHRASE CONTAINED WITHIN THE QUOTES.

"hydraulic

HMM. THAT'S STILL A LOT.

WHEN YOU GET SEVERAL SEARCH RESULTS, YOU SHOULD LOOK BEYOND JUST THE FIRST FEW. MAKE SURE TO SCROLL DOWN.

RESULTS

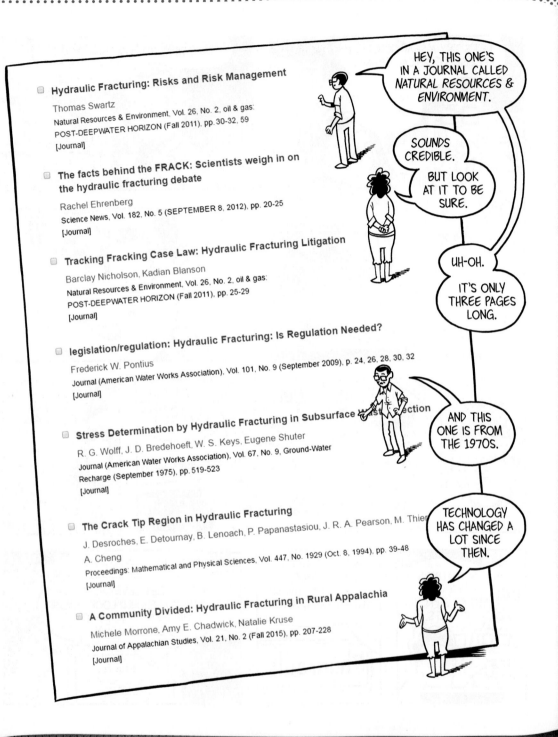

Hydraulic Fracturing: Risks and Risk Management

Thomas Swartz
Natural Resources & Environment, Vol. 26, No. 2, oil & gas:
POST-DEEPWATER HORIZON (Fall 2011), pp. 30-32, 59
[Journal]

The facts behind the FRACK: Scientists weigh in on the hydraulic fracturing debate

Rachel Ehrenberg
Science News, Vol. 182, No. 5 (SEPTEMBER 8, 2012), pp. 20-25
[Journal]

Tracking Fracking Case Law: Hydraulic Fracturing Litigation

Barclay Nicholson, Kadian Blanson
Natural Resources & Environment, Vol. 26, No. 2, oil & gas:
POST-DEEPWATER HORIZON (Fall 2011), pp. 25-29
[Journal]

legislation/regulation: Hydraulic Fracturing: Is Regulation Needed?

Frederick W. Pontius
Journal (American Water Works Association), Vol. 101, No. 9 (September 2009), p. 24, 26, 28, 30, 32
[Journal]

Stress Determination by Hydraulic Fracturing in Subsurface Waste Injection

R. G. Wolff, J. D. Bredehoeft, W. S. Keys, Eugene Shuter
Journal (American Water Works Association), Vol. 67, No. 9, Ground-Water
Recharge (September 1975), pp. 519-523
[Journal]

The Crack Tip Region in Hydraulic Fracturing

J. Desroches, E. Detournay, B. Lenoach, P. Papanastasiou, J. R. A. Pearson, M. Thiercelin, A. Cheng
Proceedings: Mathematical and Physical Sciences, Vol. 447, No. 1929 (Oct. 8, 1994), pp. 39-48
[Journal]

A Community Divided: Hydraulic Fracturing in Rural Appalachia

Michele Morrone, Amy E. Chadwick, Natalie Kruse
Journal of Appalachian Studies, Vol. 21, No. 2 (Fall 2015), pp. 207-228
[Journal]

Stress Determination by Hydraulic Fracturing in Subsurface Waste Injection

R. G. Wolff, J. D. Bredehoeft, W. S. Keys, Eugene Shuter
Journal (American Water Works Association), Vol. 67, No. 9, Ground-Water Recharge (September 1975), pp. 519-523

legislation/regulation: Hydraulic Fracturing: Is Regulation Needed?

Frederick W. Pontius
Journal (American Water Works Association), Vol. 101, No. 9 (September 2009), p. 24, 26, 28, 30, 32

TWO OF THESE ARTICLES ARE FROM A JOURNAL FROM THE AMERICAN WATER WORKS ASSOCIATION.

IT MIGHT TAKE SOME INVESTIGATING TO LEARN HOW OBJECTIVE THOSE ARTICLES ARE.

YEAH, IT'S TIME TO DIG DEEPER!

click! click! ding!

ha ha

I'M ALMOST AT THE DEPOSIT!

+ 500

ANYWAY... ...YOU CAN SEARCH JUST FOR THE PEER-REVIEWED ARTICLES FROM THAT JOURNAL, WHICH CAN BE SEPARATED FROM FEATURE ARTICLES ON WATER MANAGEMENT OR INDUSTRY NEWS.

YOU CAN ALSO DO SOME RESEARCH ON THE ORGANIZATION. HERE'S WHAT THEIR WEB SITE SAYS:

Established in 1881, the American Water Works Association is the largest nonprofit, scientific and educational association dedicated to managing and treating water, the world's most important resource.

BUT A NONPROFIT ORGANIZATION ISN'T NECESSARILY OBJECTIVE.

HOW ABOUT THIS...

251

next 50 years with current technologies. *Science* 305:968–972.
2. Tour JM, Kittrell C, Colvin VL (2010) Green carbon as a bridge to renewable energy. *Nature Mater* 9:871–874.
3. Kerr RA (2010) Natural gas from shale bursts onto the scene. *Science* 328:1624–1626.
4. Raupach MR, et al. (2007) Global and regional drivers of accelerating CO_2 emissions. *Proc Natl Acad Sci USA* 104:10288–10293.
5. US Energy Information Administration (2010) *Annual Energy Outlook 2010 with Projections to 2035* (US Energy Information Administration, Washington, DC), DOE/EIA-0383; http://www.eia.doe.gov/oiaf/aeo/pdf/0383(2010).pdf.
6. US Environmental Protection Agency (2011) Hydraulic Fracturing. (US Environmental Protection Agency, Washington, DC); http://water.epa.gov/type/groundwater/uic/class2/hydraulicfracturing/.
7. Kargbo DM, Wilhelm RG, Campbell DJ (2010) Natural gas plays in the Marcellus shale: Challenges and potential opportunities. *Environ Sci Technol* 44:5679–5684.
8. Revesz KM, Breen KJ, Baldassare AJ, Burruss RC (2010) Carbon and hydrogen isotopic evidence for the origin of combustible gases in water supply wells in north-central Pennsylvania. *Appl Geochem* 25:1845–1859.
9. Zoback M, Kitasei S, Copithorne B Addressing the environmental risks from shale gas development. *Worldwatch Institute Briefing Paper 1* (Worldwatch Inst, Washington, DC); http://blogs.worldwatch.org/revolt/wp-content/uploads/2010/07/Environmental-Risks-Paper-July-2010-FOR-PRINT.pdf.
10. Pennsylvania Department of Environmental Protection, Bureau of Oil and Gas Management (2010) 2009 Year End Workload Report. (Pennsylvania Dept of Environmental Protection, Bureau of Oil and Gas Management, Harrisburg, PA), http://www.dep.state.pa.us/dep/deputate/minres/oilgas/2009%20End%20Report-WEBSITE.pdf.
11. Colborn T, Kwiatkowski C, Schultz K, Bachran M (2010) Natural gas operations from a public health perspective. *Hum Ecol Risk Assess*, in press.
12. Pennsylvania Department of Environmental Protection (2011) Private Water Wells in Pennsylvania. (Pennsylvania Dept of Environmental Protection, Harrisburg, PA), http://www.dep.state.pa.us/dep/deputate/watermgt/wc/Subjects/SrceProt/well/.
13. Eltschlager KK, Hawkins JW, Ehler WC, Baldassare F (2001) *Technical Measures for the Investigation and Mitigation of Fugitive Methane Hazards in Areas of Coal Mining* (US Dept of the Interior, Office of Surface Mining Reclamation and Enforcement, Pittsburgh).
14. Schoell M (1980) The hydrogen and carbon isotopic composition of methane from natural gases of various origins. *Geochim Cosmochim Acta* 44:649–661.
15. Bernard BB (1978) Light hydrocarbons in marine sediments. PhD Dissertation (Texas A&M Univ, College Station, TX).
16. Jenden PD, Drazan DJ, Kaplan IR (1993) Mixing of thermogenic natural gases in northern Appalachian Basin. *Am Assoc Pet Geol Bull* 77:980–998.
17. Laughrey CD, Baldassare FJ (1998) Geochemistry and origin of some natural gases in the Plateau Province Central Appalachian Basin, Pennsylvania and Ohio. *Am Assoc Pet Geol Bull* 82:317–335.
18. Osborn SG, McIntosh JC (2010) Chemical and isotopic tracers of the contribution of microbial gas in Devonian organic-rich shales and reservoir sandstones, northern Appalachian Basin. *Appl Geochem* 25:456–471.
19. Repetski JE, Ryder RT, Harper JA, Trippi MH (2006) Thermal maturity patterns in the Ordovician and Devonian of Pennsylvania using conodont color alteration index (CAI) and vitrinite reflectance (%Ro). *Northeastern Geology Environmental Sciences*

and biogenic methane: Upper Devonia... *Cosmochim Acta* 62:1699–1720.
21. Engelder T, Lash GG, Uzcategui RS (2... Middle and Upper Devonian gas shale... *Bull* 93:857–889.
22. Pennsylvania Department of Environm... Environmental Protection, Harrisburg... pa.us/dep/deputate/minres/oilgas/new...
23. New York State Department of Health... (2009) (New York State Dept of Heal... mental Generic Environmental Statem... Well Permit Issuance for Horizontal... the Marcellus Shale and other L... riverkeeper.org/wp-content/uploads/20... 3-NYSDOH-Environmental-Radiation-M...
24. Taylor LE (1984) Groundwater Resourc... sylvania: Water Resources Report 58. ... Office of Parks and Forestry—Bureau ... PA) 139.
25. Williams JH, Taylor L, Low D (1998) H... Glaciated Valleys of Bradford, Tioga,... sources Report 68. (Commonwealth of... Resources, Harrisburg, PA) p 89.
26. Kendall C, Coplan TB (2001) Distributi... across the United States. *Hydrol Proc...*
27. Van Stempvoort D, Maathuis H, Jaw... fugitive methane in groundwater link... 43:187–199.
28. Taylor SW, Sherwood Lollar B, Wass... surface aquifers: Implications for leak... 34:4727–4732.
29. Cramer B, Schlomer S, Poelchau HS (2... the release of natural gas from groun... tions, London), 447–455.
30. Geyer AR, Wilshusen JP (1982) Engine... environmental geology supplement ... Geological Survey. (Dept of Environm... ment, Harrisburg, PA).
31. Etiope G, Martinelli G (2002) Migratio... An overview. *Phys Earth Planet Inter...*
32. Aravena R, Wassenaar LI (1993) Disso... confined aquifer, southern Ontario, C... subsurface sources. *Appl Geochem* 8:...
33. Coleman DD, Liu C, Riley KM (1988)... sediments and glacial deposits of the...
34. Alexander SS, Cakir R, Doden AG, Gold... geospatial database for Pennsylvania:... File General Geology Report 05-01.0. ... Resources, Middletown, PA), http://w...
35. Pennsylvania Spatial Data Access (PA... and gas locations. (Pennsylvania Dep... http://www.pasda.psu.edu/uci/SearchR...

31. ...e G, Martinelli G (2002) Migration of carrier a... overview. *Phys Earth Planet Inter* 129:185–204.
32. Aravena R, Wassenaar LI (1993) Dissolved organic ca... confined aquifer, southern Ontario, Canada: Carbon... subsurface sources. *Appl Geochem* 8:483–493.
33. Coleman DD, Liu C, Riley KM (1988) Microbial me... sedi... glacial deposits of the Illinois, USA. ...
34. A... ...R, Doden AG, Gold DR, Root SI (2...

COMING UP IN THE NEXT EXCITING EPISODE OF **REFRAME**

"Am I **MISSING** something?"

[pg. 279]

WALK the TALK

"RESEARCH"

1 CONNECTIONs

TO GET STARTED AS A RESEARCHER, LOOK FOR AN ENTRY POINT THAT APPEALS TO YOU. YOU CAN LOOK AT A VARIETY OF BACKGROUND SOURCES OR BEGIN WITH A PERSONAL CONNECTION THAT DRAWS YOU TO YOUR TOPIC.

MARISSA OSATO WANTED TO RESEARCH JAPANESE INTERNMENT CAMPS DURING WORLD WAR II BECAUSE OF A PERSONAL CONNECTION: HER GRANDMOTHER HAD LIVED IN ONE OF THE CAMPS.

Gesensway, Deborah, and Mindy Roseman. *Beyond Words: Images from America's Concentration Camps.* Cornell UP, 1987.

Kuramitsu, Kristine C. "Internment and Identity in Japanese American Art." *American Quarterly*, vol. 47, no. 4, Dec. 1995, pp. 619-58. *JSTOR*, doi:10.2307/2713369.

Matsuda, Ted. "Contemporary Accounts and Documents (Photocopies), 1942-1976 and Undated." Mitsuye Yamada Papers, MS-R71, Box 1, Folder 6, Special Collections and Archives, The U California Irvine Libraries, Irvine.

Osato, Mollie. Bird pins. Circa 1943-45. Photograph by Marissa Osato.

Osato, Mollie. Personal interview. 14 May 2006.

Something Strong Within. Directed by Robert A. Nakamura, Japanese American National Museum, 1994.

IDEAS AND SOURCES CAN LEAD TO UNEXPECTED PLACES. YOUR RESEARCH MIGHT EVEN END UP HELPING OTHER RESEARCHERS SOMEDAY!

SEE WHERE **YOUR** RESEARCH TAKES YOU.

DRAWING CONCLUSIONS

The following assignments ask you to practice finding, evaluating, and responding to research sources.

1 Look at Liz's detective map on p. 221. Try to follow the arrows and construct a version of her investigation, writing out a step-by-step narrative that describes the process.

Think about the organization of your details, and craft a story that makes some kind of sense even when the illustrations are outlandish.

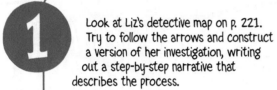

2 Choose a current event that you already know a little bit about, and spend some time gathering what you believe are unreliable resources on that topic -- perhaps a biased news site or a personal blog.

Once you've gathered some examples, try to think of instances in which these resources might be useful, depending on what aspect of the event is being discussed.

On the other end of the spectrum, are there ever instances when "reputable" sources of information might **NOT** be suitable for a particular piece of writing?

3 Choose a historical event and search for as many different kinds of sources on the topic as you can -- primary and secondary, fiction and nonfiction, multimedia, digital, etc.

As you gather your list, brainstorm ways you can evaluate the usefulness or relevance of each source. What are your methods for finding different sources? What kinds of sources are easier or more difficult to find?

4 A good way to begin creating a research-based argument is to find a position that you will refute or critique. Think about your position on some significant aspect of the event you began researching in question 3.

Find a source that takes a thoughtful position that differs from your own. Summarize that source's argument fairly, and then sketch out a chart or an outline of your response.

THAT'S NOT WHAT WE WANT TO SHOW PEOPLE ABOUT **REVISION**.

YEAH, REVISION ISN'T JUST ABOUT CORRECTING **MISTAKES**.

IT MEANS EXACTLY WHAT IT SAYS:

"RE-VISION."

IT'S ABOUT SEEING A COMPOSITION ANEW, WITH FRESH EYES --

-- SEEING YOUR OWN WORK AS IF YOU WERE ANOTHER READER.

IT'S ABOUT CONSIDERING POSSIBILITIES...

...AS WELL AS PROBLEMS.

LOOKING FOR ERRORS THAT ARE DISTRACTING, EVEN IF THEY DON'T SERIOUSLY INTERFERE WITH READERS' UNDERSTANDING, IS ONLY THE MOST BASIC FORM OF REVISION.

BUT EVEN IF FLAWS AREN'T SERIOUS, THEY CAN MAKE YOU LOOK **TERRIBLE.**

YOU CAN'T JUST IGNORE WHAT EVERYONE CAN SEE PLAINLY.

PEOPLE MIGHT NOT SAY ANY-THING TO YOUR FACE, BUT THEY WILL CERTAINLY JUDGE YOU IF YOU LOOK BAD.

SO-CALLED "SURFACE ERRORS" CAN BE A TURN-OFF TO AUDIENCES.

LIKE ITS AND IT'S. WHY CAN'T PEOPLE GET THAT RIGHT?

OR THEIR, THEY'RE, AND THERE.

I HATE THAT MISTAKE.

LOOK, WE UNDERSTAND.

WE'RE WRITING TEACHERS. WE SEE MISTAKES ALL DAY LONG.

PLEASE COME AGAIN

FASHION!

POP! POP!

SOME COMMON ERRORS ARE ALSO VERY DISTRACTING.

OUR FRIEND ELLEN STRENSKI CALLS THESE "NOSE-PICKING ERRORS."

SUCH ERRORS SEEM TO INDICATE A LACK OF SELF-AWARENESS.

AND THEY SIGNAL THAT THE PEOPLE WHO MAKE THEM EITHER DON'T KNOW CONVENTIONS OF ACADEMIC WRITING OR WON'T SHOW THEIR AUDIENCES ENOUGH RESPECT TO EDIT THE WORK CAREFULLY.

SOME PEOPLE FIND THESE ERRORS SO REPULSIVE THAT THEY CAN'T PAY ATTENTION TO THE MESSAGE BEING DELIVERED.

THESE PEOPLE MAY BE OVERLY SENSITIVE ABOUT IMPERFECTION...

CENSORED

...BUT YOU WANT TO AVOID UNINTENTIONALLY CREATING STRONG NEGATIVE REACTIONS TO YOUR WRITING.

...IS IT OVER?

THAT WAS **HORRIBLE**.

SNEAK SNEAK

GOTCHA!

SEE, NOW HE LOOKS MUCH MORE PRESENTABLE.

NOW NO ONE WILL BE ABLE TO TELL THAT ANYTHING IS WRONG.

MURPH!

BUT YOU AREN'T ACTUALLY ADDRESSING HIS UNDERLYING PROBLEMS.

YOU'RE JUST TRYING TO COVER UP ANY SYMPTOMS THAT SOMETHING IS WRONG.

GOOD WRITING TEACHERS ENCOURAGE THEIR STUDENTS TO ADDRESS BIG-PICTURE ISSUES...

...NOT JUST IRRITATING LITTLE MISTAKES.

PRETTY MUCH ALL OF THE BOOKS IN THIS LIBRARY WERE REVISED DURING THE DRAFTING PROCESS IN WAYS THAT WENT FAR BEYOND SIMPLY FIXING SPELLING AND GRAMMATICAL MISTAKES.

SEE THIS BOOK?

IT'S *PERSUASION,* JANE AUSTEN'S LAST NOVEL. THE INITIAL DRAFT OF THIS BOOK HAD A COMPLETELY DIFFERENT ENDING.

THE ORIGINAL ENDING DIDN'T HAVE THE WITTY DIALOGUE OR THE OBSERVATIONS ABOUT HUMAN CHARACTER THAT AUSTEN WAS KNOWN FOR.

THE FIRST VERSION OF AUSTEN'S HAPPY ENDING COMES ABOUT BECAUSE THE HEROINE IS TRICKED INTO BEING ALONE WITH THE HERO. WHEN HE DECLARES HIS LOVE FOR HER IN VERY CONVENTIONAL LANGUAGE, SHE DOESN'T HAVE MUCH TO SAY IN RESPONSE.

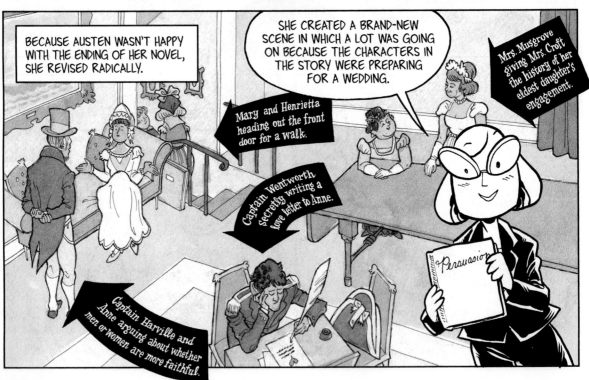

BECAUSE AUSTEN WASN'T HAPPY WITH THE ENDING OF HER NOVEL, SHE REVISED RADICALLY.

SHE CREATED A BRAND-NEW SCENE IN WHICH A LOT WAS GOING ON BECAUSE THE CHARACTERS IN THE STORY WERE PREPARING FOR A WEDDING.

Mary and Henrietta heading out the front door for a walk.

Captain Wentworth secretly writing a love letter to Anne.

Mrs. Musgrove giving Mrs. Croft the history of her eldest daughter's engagement.

Captain Harville and Anne arguing about whether men or women are more faithful.

Persuasion

IN THE REVISED ENDING, AUSTEN'S HEROINE SHOWS HERSELF TO BE A SOPHISTICATED CONVERSATIONALIST IN A DEBATE ABOUT WHETHER MEN OR WOMEN ARE MORE FAITHFUL IN LOVE.

ALTHOUGH HE DOESN'T SEEM TO BE PAYING ATTENTION, THE DASHING HERO IS ACTUALLY LISTENING TO HER ARGUMENT ATTENTIVELY.

WHILE ALL THE ACTION IS GOING ON AROUND HIM, HE WRITES HER A LETTER TO TELL HER HOW HE REALLY FEELS.

I DEFINITELY LIKE THAT ENDING BETTER.

IT IS A LOT MORE RHETORICALLY INTERESTING.

OF COURSE, A MORE ELABORATE SOLUTION TO A PROBLEM IN A PIECE OF WRITING ISN'T ALWAYS THE RIGHT APPROACH.

SOMETIMES A SIMPLER SOLUTION IS BETTER.

TEMPUS FUGIT

BUT WHETHER YOU'RE REVISING A NOVEL OR A PIECE OF ACADEMIC WRITING...

...IT'S IMPORTANT TO GIVE YOURSELF ENOUGH TIME TO MAKE MAJOR REVISIONS, AS AUSTEN DID.

SEWARD WAS RIGHT TO BE WORRIED. LINCOLN'S EARLY DRAFTS FOR THE INAUGURAL ADDRESS WERE EXTREMELY CONFRONTATIONAL.

In your hands, my dissatisfied fellow countrymen, and not in mine, is the momentous issue of civil war. The government will not assail you, unless you first assail it. You can have no conflict, without being yourselves the aggressors. You have no oath registered in Heaven to destroy the government, while I shall have the most solemn one to "preserve, protect, and defend" it. You can forbear the assault upon it; I can not shrink from the defense of it. With you, and not with me, is the solemn question of "Shall it be peace, or a sword?"

HE'S PRACTICALLY DARING SLAVEHOLDING STATES TO REVOLT.

"SHALL IT BE PEACE, OR A SWORD?" WHAT A TERRIBLE ENDING!

WHAT IS HE **THINKING**?

SEWARD LATER EXPLAINED WHAT HE SAW AS THE FLAW IN LINCOLN'S ORIGINAL APPROACH:

...we must CHANGE THE QUESTION BEFORE THE PUBLIC FROM ONE UPON SLAVERY, OR ABOUT SLAVERY, for a question upon UNION OR DISUNION.

SEWARD KNEW THAT THE FINAL WORDS OF THE SPEECH WERE GOING TO HAVE THE MOST RHETORICAL IMPACT. SO HE OFFERED THE PRESIDENT SOME DIFFERENT OPTIONS FOR WORDING AND SUGGESTED TWO DIFFERENT ENDINGS.

LIKE ANY GOOD PEER REVIEWER, SEWARD GAVE HIS PARTNER SOME CHOICES.

LINCOLN LIKED THE SECOND OF SEWARD'S SUGGESTED CLOSING PARAGRAPHS BETTER.

The mystic chords which proceeding from so many battle fields and so many patriot graves pass through all the hearts and all the hearths in this broad continent of ours will yet again harmonize in their ancient music when breathed upon by the guardian angel of the nation.

LINCOLN APPROVED OF SEWARD'S COMPLEX METAPHOR OF A MUSICAL STRING CONNECTING TWO POINTS.

THIS RHETORICAL FIGURE REPRESENTED THE EMOTIONAL BOND CONNECTING THE GRAVES OF REVOLUTIONARY SOLDIERS TO THE PEOPLE OF LINCOLN'S OWN DAY.

We are not enemies, but friends.
We must not be enemies.

Though passion may have strained, it must not break our bonds of affection.

The mystic chords of memory, stretching from every battlefield, and patriot grave, to every living heart and hearthstone, all over this broad land, will yet swell the chorus of the Union, when again touched, as surely they will be, by the better angels of our nature.

WHEN YOUR OWN WORK IS REVIEWED BY OTHER PEOPLE, IT CAN BE IMPORTANT TO EVALUATE THEIR SUGGESTIONS.

ACCEPTING ALL ADVICE FROM OTHERS UNCRITICALLY CAN BE ALMOST AS BAD AS REFUSING TO LISTEN TO FEEDBACK IN THE FIRST PLACE.

BE AN ACTIVE PARTICIPANT IN YOUR REVISION PROCESS AT EVERY STAGE OF DRAFTING.

WE ENCOURAGE YOU TO THINK ABOUT REVISION RADICALLY.

SOMETIMES WRITERS HAVE TO MAKE RADICAL REVISIONS FOR REASONS NOT OF THEIR OWN CHOOSING.

TONIGHT: 7pm Maxine Hong Kingston

WHEN THE MANUSCRIPT OF WRITER MAXINE HONG KINGSTON'S NOVEL-IN-PROGRESS BURNED IN 1991, ALONG WITH HER HOUSE AND ALL HER POSSESSIONS, SHE HAD TO RECONSTITUTE MATERIAL FROM MEMORY. SHE CHOSE TO INCORPORATE THE STORY OF THE FIRE INTO THE FINAL VERSION OF HER NOVEL, CALLED *THE FIFTH BOOK OF PEACE.*

OF COURSE, THIS EXPERIENCE WAS TRAUMATIC FOR KINGSTON.

BUT IT ALSO SHOWS HOW DESTRUCTION MAY SOMETIMES BE A PART OF THE CREATIVE PROCESS.

YOU MIGHT ASK YOURSELF:

IF I COULD ONLY SAVE ONE PARAGRAPH OF THE WORK I'M WRITING, WHICH ONE WOULD I SAVE?

WHICH ONE WOULD I LET GO FIRST?

Cutting and pasting text on a computer screen may seem monotonous, so you might try printing out your work and physically moving the pieces...

AS YOU REVISE, THINK ABOUT WHETHER THE CHOICES YOU'RE MAKING IN THIS WRITING PROJECT FOLLOW THE RHETORICAL ADVICE IN OTHER CHAPTERS OF THIS BOOK.

PAY ATTENTION TO THE APPEALS TO ETHOS, LOGOS, AND PATHOS* IN THE WORK THAT YOU COMPOSE.

*For more on these appeals, see CHAPTER 1.

DO YOUR RHETORICAL CHOICES PRESENT YOU AS A TRUSTWORTHY WRITER?

IS YOUR REASONING PRESENTED LOGICALLY?

ARE YOU ATTENTIVE TO HOW YOU MOVE THE EMOTIONS OF YOUR AUDIENCE?

HOW WILL YOUR WORK BE READ BY A READER VERY DIFFERENT FROM YOURSELF*?

THINK ABOUT THAT PERSON'S EXPECTATIONS CAREFULLY.

*For more on ideal readers, see CHAPTER 2.

DOES YOUR OWN READING OF THE SOURCES THAT YOU INCORPORATE REPRESENT YOUR BEST ANALYTICAL WORK?

REMEMBER, DON'T KEEP YOUR IDENTITY* A SECRET IF YOU WANT TO SAVE THE WORLD WITH YOUR WRITING.

*For more on identity, see CHAPTER 3.

*For more on argument, see CHAPTER 4.

*For more on collaboration, see CHAPTER 5.

YOU MIGHT THINK IT'S TOO LATE TO KEEP INVESTIGATING, BUT RESEARCH* IS AN IMPORTANT PART OF THE REVISION PROCESS.

ARE THERE ANY SOURCES THAT YOU HAVE OVERLOOKED?

ARE THERE ANY SOURCES THAT CAN'T BE TRUSTED?

AND HAVE YOU CREDITED ALL THE DETECTIVE WORK THAT ISN'T YOUR OWN?

*For more on research, see CHAPTER 6.

SOMETIMES IT IS HELPFUL TO FOCUS ON **ADDING**. ARE THERE PARTS OF THE ARGUMENT THAT SEEM UNDERDEVELOPED?

READ YOUR DRAFT AND THINK ABOUT WHAT QUESTIONS YOUR WRITING POSES -- YOU CAN EVEN WRITE THEM IN THE MARGINS.

DO ANY OF THESE QUESTIONS NEED TO BE ANSWERED?

IF SO, YOU MAY NEED TO DO FURTHER THINKING OR RESEARCH.

CHECK YOUR SOURCES CAREFULLY.

HAVE YOU CITED EVERYTHING THAT NEEDS TO BE CITED?

ARE YOUR IN-TEXT AND BIBLIOGRAPHIC CITATIONS IN ORDER?

REMEMBER THAT YOU SHOULD INVEST TIME IN READING YOUR OWN WORK CRITICALLY.

Issue 7 • Rethinking Revision

REFRAME with Luis & Cindy

Am I MISSING something?

"HEY, CINDY, WHAT'S UP?"
WRITING CENTER

"WELL, I JUST MET WITH THE INSTRUCTOR FOR MY ART HISTORY CLASS, AND NOW I NEED HELP."

"SEE, IT'S --"

YANK!
"WAIT A MINUTE..."

"...YOU'RE COMING TO THE WRITING CENTER FOR AN **ART HISTORY** PAPER?"

"YES, OF COURSE!"
"JONATHAN SAID WE COULD TAKE **ANY** KIND OF WRITING TO THE WRITING CENTER -- NOT JUST ENGLISH PAPERS."

!
YANK BACK!

"SIGH..."

"AND MY INSTRUCTOR SAYS I HAVE TO REVISE THE **WHOLE** PROJECT."

WRITING CENTER

"FINE. HERE."
WRITING CENTER

"Since the dawn of time, art has made the expression of ideas and feelings possible.

This makes art a hugely important part of all human life.

Art even appears in caves that were visited by ancient humans, and art remains an important part of basically every culture everywhere around the globe . . ."

WELL, LET'S START AT THE BEGINNING. DO YOU HAVE THE PROMPT FOR THE ASSIGNMENT?

I TOOK SOME NOTES WHEN THE INSTRUCTOR GAVE THE ASSIGNMENT. SHE WANTS US TO "SPECULATE ON WHAT CAVE PAINTINGS SUGGEST ABOUT PRIMITIVE CULTURES."

HERE WE GO.

LET'S SEE WHAT YOU'VE GOT SO FAR.

HMM...

YOUR READERS ALREADY UNDERSTAND THAT ART IS IMPORTANT. YOU DON'T NEED TO BEGIN WITH SUCH A BROAD SET OF ASSERTIONS.

WHAT "DIFFERENT PEOPLE" WILL YOU BE TALKING ABOUT IN THIS ESSAY?

WELL, A LOT OF CAVE PAINTINGS COME FROM CULTURES OF HUNTERS AND GATHERERS.

I GUESS MY INSTRUCTOR WANTS ME TO FOCUS ON **THEIR** IDEAS...

OK, GOOD. WHAT IDEAS?

HMM. WHAT IDEAS WOULD BE IMPORTANT TO THAT KIND OF CULTURE?

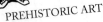

PREHISTORIC ART

Since the dawn of time, art has made the expression of ideas and feelings possible. This makes art a hugely important part of all human life. Art even appears in caves that were visited by ancient humans, and art remains an important part of basically every culture everywhere around the globe. Different people have different ideas about what makes art important or valuable, and about why works of art like cave paintings were created in the first place and how they can best be preserved for future generations. But many people agree that art is one of the ingredients that contributes to making life worth living. In this essay, I will examine the views of several important art historians about cave art and analyze where I stand on these questions.

MAYBE I SHOULD SPECULATE ON WHY SO MANY CAVE ARTISTS CHOSE TO SHOW IMAGES OF **ANIMALS**-- BUT NOT **PEOPLE**.

AND IMAGES OF **REAL** CAVE ART WOULD BE A BETTER WAY TO ILLUSTRATE MY ARGUMENT.

I REALLY THINK YOU'RE ON TO SOMETHING INTERESTING--

--AND PROBABLY GETTING CLOSER TO WHAT YOUR INSTRUCTOR IS ASKING YOU TO THINK ABOUT.

I COULD START BY FOCUSING ON IMAGES OF BISON, WHICH WERE IMPORTANT AS FOOD.

BISON PROVIDED HIDES, TOO, AND EVEN THEIR BONES COULD BE MADE INTO TOOLS. BISON WERE A BIG PART OF THAT CULTURE.

THAT SOUNDS LIKE A MUCH BETTER START-ING POINT.

OK, I'VE GOT SOME **REVISING** TO DO...

...I THINK I SEE THIS WHOLE THING IN A **NEW WAY!**

COMING UP IN THE NEXT EXCITING EPISODE OF **REFRAME**

"How does this LOOK?"

[pg. 311]

285

DRAWING CONCLUSIONS

The following assignments ask you to
think about your revision process.

1 List the best and worst revision advice you've ever received. You might consider your experiences revising writing or essays, photoshopping images, creating graphic designs, or even developing a piece of art or craft work.

Next, draft a set of "best practices for responding to my work," and turn it into a publishable format and genre that you can distribute to the next person you share your work with. You might write a letter, create a wallet-sized "peer response guide," design an infographic, or create a short video or Web site whose URL you can hand out.

2 Create a reverse outline of an essay by highlighting the thesis statement and writing one-sentence summaries of the key argument each paragraph makes. Write down what you know about the author and the audience for the essay.

Next, create "characters" out of the author and an audience member. Write a short dialogue in which the author tries to convince the audience member of his or her claim using only the one-sentence paragraph summaries as arguments. Is your audience character convinced? If not, what argument points fall flat, or what additional information does the author character need to provide? Does the audience character introduce new counterarguments that your author character might need to address?

3

Maxine Hong Kingston was once forced to radically and dramatically revise a draft of her novel after it was burned in a house fire. Fortunately, there are less tragic and more controlled ways to simulate this sort of revision.

Print out your essay, read through it, and then seal it in an envelope. Walk away for a short break, and when you get back to your work space, try to reconstruct the essay from memory. Print out that version, unseal the envelope, and compare the two drafts.

Choose the best parts from each draft, and weave them together to make an improved, revised draft.

4

Choose one paragraph, from your own writing or from something you're reading, and take inventory of the contents: Are the sentences mostly long or short? Are there more simple, compound, or complex sentences in the paragraph?

Then rewrite the paragraph a few different ways. Combine sentences so that all the sentences are long. How does that change the experience of reading the paragraph? Is it more or less accessible to the reader? Does it change the tone of the piece?

Next, rewrite the paragraph using only short and simple sentences. What effect does that change have on the text? Keep experimenting with a number of variables: rewriting from a different perspective (from third-person to first-person, for instance), rewriting with all active or all passive voice sentences, and so on. Write a brief analysis of the effects of each change.

LAUNCHING INTO THE FUTURE OF GENRES

BEFORE WE TALK ABOUT PUTTING WORK IN FRONT OF AN AUDIENCE, WE THOUGHT WE'D TAKE A LITTLE BREAK FROM WRITING.

WE BOTH ENJOY FILM A GREAT DEAL.

DRAMA, COMEDY, ROMANCE, HORROR, WESTERN, SCIENCE FICTION, ACTION/ADVENTURE, MYSTERY, THRILLER...

THERE ARE MANY DIFFERENT CATEGORIES TO CHOOSE FROM.

AUDIENCES EXPECT DIFFERENT THINGS FROM DIFFERENT GENRES.

AND EACH GENRE IS A UNIQUE EXPERIENCE, WITH DIFFERENT CONVENTIONS AND EXPECTATIONS.

HEY--

I THOUGHT WE WERE SEEING A SCIENCE FICTION FILM TODAY...

...BUT I'M IN THE MOOD FOR A ROMANTIC COMEDY.

AS YOU CAN SEE, GENRE OFTEN SETS THE STAGE IN DETERMINING HOW AUDIENCES WILL APPROACH A FILM -- OR A PIECE OF WRITING.

UH-OH.

BEAMED INTO SPACE!!

HELP!

FOR INSTANCE, THE GENRE OF SCIENCE FICTION MIGHT EVOKE OUTER SPACE, NON-HUMAN CREATURES, OR LIFE IN A HIGH-TECH FUTURE.

WE LEARN THE CONVENTIONS OF DIFFERENT GENRES AS WE'RE EXPOSED TO THEM.

HUMAN F

BEAM

BEAMED INTO SPACE!

WE'RE USED TO CATEGORIZING FILM ACCORDING TO GENRE, BUT GENRE IS AT WORK **EVERYWHERE.**

BOOT!

FOR INSTANCE...

...THERE ARE FITNESS MAGAZINES...

...AND COOKING MAGAZINES...

...AND TECHNOLOGY MAGAZINES.

DIFFERENT GENRES CALL FOR DIFFERENT RHETORICAL CHOICES.

EVERYTHING WE SEE -- FROM WORD CHOICE TO DESIGN -- TELLS US WHAT TO EXPECT.

AUDIENCES FOR A NEWSMAGAZINE EXPECT TRUSTWORTHY STORIES NOT INFLUENCED BY ADVERTISERS.

SO IT'S IMPORTANT FOR THE STORIES TO BE DESIGNED DIFFERENTLY FROM THE ADS.

BUT IN A SCIENCE FICTION MAGAZINE...

...TELLING THE ADS FROM THE ARTICLES PROBABLY DOESN'T MATTER AS MUCH TO READERS.

CERTAIN GENRES ARE COMMON IN ACADEMIC WRITING. YOU MIGHT WRITE JOURNAL ENTRIES OR EDIT MATERIAL FROM ORAL INTERVIEWS...

...OR COMPOSE LAB REPORTS FOR SCIENCE COURSES.

ACADEMIC DISCIPLINES OFTEN PREFER PARTICULAR GENRES THAT SET UP EXPECTATIONS FOR READERS.

PAN-GALACTIC TELECONFERENCE

BIOLOGY NEBULA

LITERATURE ASTEROID

ART GALAXY

A LAB REPORT, FOR INSTANCE, MAY BEGIN WITH BACKGROUND INFORMATION, A LITERATURE REVIEW...

...AND A METHODOLOGY SECTION THAT EXPLAINS HOW THE EXPERIMENTER PROCEEDED.

THIS CONVENTIONAL FORMAT PROVIDES INFORMATION THAT SCIENTISTS EXPECT TO KNOW BEFORE THEY READ THE RESULTS OF THE EXPERIMENT.

JOURNAL of COOL SCIENCE

LAB NOTES

AN ANALYSIS OF A **POEM**, IN CONTRAST...

...MIGHT NOT BEGIN WITH A SEPARATE BACKGROUND SECTION, BUT THE WRITER MIGHT BRING UP INFORMATION ABOUT THE POET'S LIFE OR OTHER CONTEXT WHEN ANALYZING PARTICULAR LINES.

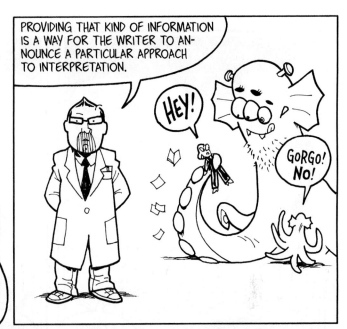

PROVIDING THAT KIND OF INFORMATION IS A WAY FOR THE WRITER TO ANNOUNCE A PARTICULAR APPROACH TO INTERPRETATION.

HEY!

GORGO! NO!

SO, THERE'S A **METHOD** EVEN IN THE MADNESS OF POETRY ANALYSIS!

DESIGN

MEDIUM

SUBJECT MATTER

TONE

FORMAT

CHOICE

LEVEL of LANGUAGE

SOME GENRES THAT ARE DESIGNED FOR PARTICULAR PURPOSES AND AUDIENCES...

BUT THE FORMATS OF A LITERARY ANALYSIS AND A LAB REPORT WILL TYPICALLY BE VERY DIFFERENT.

...MAY SEEM PRETTY ALIEN TO OUTSIDERS.

HELP!

ENGLISH PROFESSOR

...INTERROGATING THE CONDITIONS OF SYSTEMATICITY...

I CAN'T UNDERSTAND YOU.

BIOLOGY PROFESSOR

...AIJ = DIJ = 0 IF THE QTL IS NOT SEGREGATING IN CROSS I...

IT'S LIKE YOU'RE FROM A DIFFERENT PLANET.

TO WORK IN A GENRE, YOU SHOULD UNDERSTAND ITS EXPECTED CONVENTIONS -- THE WAY IT COMMUNICATES KNOWLEDGE.

DIFFERENCES AMONG GENRES SOMETIMES SIGNAL DIFFERENCES IN HOW WRITERS IN DIFFERENT DISCIPLINES APPROACH...

AAAAH!

HE'S GONE NUTS!

...OR EVEN THINK ABOUT A SUBJECT.

HELP!

SO, DIFFERENT WAYS OF PRESENTING DIFFERENT TYPES OF KNOWLEDGE RESULT IN...

...DIFFERENT GENRES!

PLOP

?!

NAVIGATING AMONG MEDIA

WE CAN SEE GENRE CONVENTIONS AT PLAY IN MANY ONLINE SPACES.

LIZLOSH @JONATHANALEX243
brrow yr top hat?

LOL no I need it!

http://www.bigtimehats.com/formalwear
FOR SALE:
One top hat $50.00 BUY!

THINK ABOUT THE LAYOUT OF THE SCREEN AND WHAT EXPECTATIONS YOU MIGHT WANT TO FULFILL WHEN WRITING IN A DIGITAL GENRE.

FOR INSTANCE, AN EMAIL USUALLY HAS A GREETING...

Hi, Liz--

...WHILE A TEXT MESSAGE ONLY HAS A GREETING SOMETIMES...

...AND A WEB PAGE DOESN'T HAVE A GREETING BECAUSE IT'S NOT ADDRESSED TO A SPECIFIC PERSON.

AND WHILE EACH OF THESE WRITING SPACES -- EMAIL, WEB PAGES, TEXTS -- CAN HAVE ITS OWN GENRE CONVENTIONS, EACH CAN ALSO ACCOMMODATE A WIDE VARIETY OF GENRES.

FOR EXAMPLE, BLOGS AND WIKIS ARE WEB GENRES THAT ARE ALSO COLLABORATIVE WRITING SPACES.

LIZ IS THE PRIMARY AUTHOR OF HER BLOG, *VIRTUALPOLITIK*, AND JONATHAN CAN MAKE COMMENTS.

ARTICLES ON WIKIPEDIA OFTEN HAVE MORE THAN ONE PRIMARY AUTHOR.

BARGE IN!

IN EACH CASE, THE GENRE ESTABLISHES EXPECTATIONS FOR HOW PEOPLE SHOULD CONVERSE ON THE SITE.

301

...IT ALSO **MOVES**.

IT CHANGES SHAPE, FORM, AND FUNCTION DEPENDING ON WHAT WE'RE COMMUNICATING, TO WHOM, AND HOW.

SOMETIMES SIMILAR IDEAS MAY BE PUBLISHED IN VERY DIFFERENT KINDS OF WORK.

ERRT

WHOA, IT'S **GREG BENFORD**, ACADEMIC PHYSICIST AND SCIENCE FICTION WRITER!

HE'S WRITTEN ABOUT THE GALACTIC CENTER IN NOVELS AND ALSO IN ACADEMIC PAPERS.

303

BUT *PUBLISHING* JUST MEANS GOING PUBLIC WITH YOUR WORK, AND YOU DON'T NEED TO BE A BOOK AUTHOR TO EXPERIENCE THAT THRILL.

YIKES!

SHWOOSH!!!

THANK YOU!

WRITING MORPHS AND CHANGES MEANING AS IT MOVES FROM ONE MEDIUM OR GENRE OR RHETORICAL SITUATION TO ANOTHER.

YOU'VE SEEN THIS MOVEMENT AS YOU'VE TRAVELED WITH US THROUGH THE COURSE OF THIS BOOK.

AND WRITING MOVES TOWARD AUDIENCES -- SOMETIMES SPECIFIC AND INTENDED AUDIENCES, AND SOMETIMES UNINTENDED AUDIENCES.

AS WRITING GETS **READ**, OTHER PEOPLE CAN RESPOND.

A HIGH-SPEED EXCHANGE OF INFORMATION CAN BE THRILLING...

...WITH DIGITAL GENRES MAKING NEW FORMS OF AUTHORSHIP AVAILABLE TO WRITERS WHO MIGHT NEVER FIND AUDIENCES OTHERWISE...

BURMA SHAVE

...AND WITH INFORMATION DISSEMINATED AS QUICKLY AS IT IS PRODUCED AND CONSUMED --

WAIT, WERE YOU SPEEDING?

IT'S TRUE, MY FRIENDS.

TEXTUAL AND VISUAL MATERIAL IS CONSTANTLY ON THE MOVE...

...BEING RETASKED AND REPURPOSED FOR A VARIETY OF MEDIA...

...BUT YOU HAVE TO PAY ATTENTION TO WHAT YOU'RE DOING, OR YOU'LL END UP PULLED OVER TO THE SIDE OF THE INFORMATION SUPERHIGHWAY.

SPEEDING TICKET

YES INDEED, YOU HAVE TO PLOT YOUR COURSE CAREFULLY...

...AND MAKE SURE ALL THE GEARS OF YOUR MEDIUM AND MESSAGE FIT TOGETHER PERFECTLY, SO THAT YOUR WRITING DOESN'T...

...UHHH...

...ROCKET OFF IN THE WRONG DIRECTION...

Learning to See Writing

📷 Blog Post created by **Jonathan Alexander** 🐤 on Nov 7, 2016

[Speech bubble:] YOU'RE ABSOLUTELY RIGHT.

[Speech bubble:] SEE, HERE'S A POST ABOUT RHETORIC FOR A BLOG AIMED AT AN AUDIENCE OF COMPOSITION TEACHERS.

...r me, one of the biggest challenges of working on a graphic book has been adapting to thinking and composing in a different ...um. Indeed, one of the lessons we have learned in the process is that we can't just think like "text" authors; we also have to begin to ...sually. As we sketch out the chapters, panel by panel, we try to provide detailed visual cues for Kevin Cannon and Zander Cannon, ...ulous artists–who, in turn, not only modify our initial image directions and augment them beautifully, but have also challenged how ...erstand and use text in the graphic book form.

...g these lines, one of the earliest lessons we learned about our use of text is that we were initially relying too much ...captioning and not enough on dialogue to carry the instructional weight of each chapter. That is, we were thinking ...ke the text-producing scholars that we are, and not like the collaborative graphic authors we needed to be. We were constantly explaining rhetorical concepts, for instance, while ignoring how images and dialogue—the principal features of the comic form—could be used to convey our ideas about writing. Comparing initial drafts of the first several chapters with their more recent revisions shows a steady move away from captioning to significantly more reliance on dialogue ...s.

...itant with that shift has been a shift in how we think about the project and the pr... ...aximize our use of the comic form. For instance, we've frequently found ourselve... ...g dialogue out loud to make sure that our characters strike the right—and cre... ...ue format forced us to focus on the process of understanding rhetorical conce... ...on, coming to understand concepts such as logos and ethos, or the complexi... ...ess. The format of the comic book allows us—actually requires us—to model, di... ...ns to compose.

[Speech bubble:] AND HERE'S A PANEL FROM THIS BOOK ABOUT THE SAME TOPIC. THIS ONE'S AIMED AT STUDENTS, AND IT USES A PRINT MEDIUM WITH A LOT OF VISUALS, A COMIC BOOK, TO MAKE THE POINT.

...on this particular example of how our composing process had to shift because it seems to... ...reminder of how different genres call forth different modalities of thinking, as Anis Bawarshi argues in *Genre and* ...e *Invention of the Writer* :

[Caption, rotated:] (Photo) Mack McCoy

[Thought bubble:] I WONDER WHAT THOSE STUDENTS ARE LAUGHING ABOUT?

[Speech bubble:] JUST ADDING WORDS CAN CHANGE THE ENTIRE MEANING OF AN IMAGE.

AHH!

YOU SEEM TO RECOGNIZE ALREADY THAT THE FORMATS AND GENRES THROUGH WHICH WE ENCOUNTER TEXTS ARE THEMSELVES IN MOTION, ACCOMMODATING NEW WAYS OF RECEIVING-- AND DISSEMINATING-- INFORMATION!

EXPERTS CALL THAT **REMEDIATION.**

THAT'S RIGHT!

TEXT IS ALWAYS ON THE MOVE.

MAYBE HUNDREDS OF YEARS FROM NOW, PEOPLE WILL BE REMIXING THE TEXTS, IMAGES, AND SOUNDS WE CREATE TODAY IN TOTALLY DIFFERENT WAYS.

YOU BET!

THOSE PICTURES YOU PUT ON THAT SOCIAL NETWORK SITE, FOR INSTANCE...

309

REFRAME with Luis & Cindy

How does this LOOK?

HEY, LUIS.

HEY, CINDY!

HEY, CINDY'S MOM!

ISN'T THIS MEDIA LAB **AWESOME**?

YEAH, I'M DOING MORE AND MORE MEDIA PROJECTS FOR MY CLASSES, SO IT'S NICE TO HAVE ALL THIS SOFTWARE...

SO, WHAT ARE YOU GUYS UP TO?

I'M HELPING MY MOM LEARN TO MAKE PRESENTATION SLIDES.

SHE'S WORKING ON A PROJECT FOR **HER** WRITING CLASS.

COMPUTERS AREN'T MY THING, BUT I'M ACTUALLY HAVING A GOOD TIME ANYWAY...

YEAH, I'M WORKING ON A PRESENTATION TOO...FOR MY RESEARCH PROJECT ON FORCED MIGRATION.

I'M WRITING ABOUT PEOPLE WHO COME TO THE UNITED STATES BECAUSE THEIR LIVES ARE IN DANGER IN THEIR HOME COUNTRIES.

HEY, REMEMBER HOW I TOLD YOU THAT MY MOTHER LEFT VIETNAM AS A BOAT PERSON?

SHE CAME TO THIS COUNTRY BECAUSE OF FORCED MIGRATION.

HER UNCLE HAD ALREADY BEEN EXECUTED BY THE COMMUNISTS. HER OLDER BROTHER HAD BEEN A TRANSLATOR FOR THE U.S. MILITARY, SO THE WHOLE FAMILY HAD TO LEAVE.

I ALWAYS TELL MY DAUGHTER HOW LUCKY SHE IS.

I LIVED IN A REFUGEE CAMP WHEN I WAS HER AGE!

HMM...

REC

WOULD YOU MIND IF I INTERVIEWED YOU FOR MY PROJECT?

IT WOULD BE GREAT TO HAVE AN EYEWITNESS REPORT!

AND SO...

BUT HOW WILL YOU INCLUDE A VIDEO IN YOUR PAPER?

WELL...

...FOR OUR RESEARCH PROJECTS, WE HAVE TO WRITE A PAPER AND THEN CREATE A MULTIMEDIA PRESENTATION ON THE SAME SUBJECT.

LIZ WANTS US TO CHOOSE A SPECIFIC CASE STUDY, SO I COULD WRITE ABOUT FORCED MIGRATION FROM VIETNAM TO THE UNITED STATES.

FMC

About Contact

Forced Migration Online: Resources f
Ongoing Study and Research

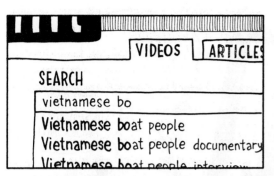

VIDEOS | ARTICLES

SEARCH

vietnamese bo

Vietnamese boat people

Vietnamese boat people documentary

Vietnamese boat people interview

BY THE END OF THE TERM, WE HAVE TO COMBINE ALL OUR WORK INTO ONE COHERENT PROJECT...

...SO I THINK I'M GOING TO MAKE A WEB SITE WHERE I CAN POST MY PAPER ON VIETNAMESE REFUGEES AND ALSO LINK TO VIDEO AND IMAGES AND DOCUMENTS THAT I COLLECT.

AN INTERVIEW CAN BE A REALLY POWERFUL SOURCE.

CAROL, WOULD YOU TALK ABOUT WHAT IT FELT LIKE TO LIVE THROUGH FORCED MIGRATION?

I'D BE FLATTERED TO BE INCLUDED.

GREAT! I'LL THINK OF SOME QUESTIONS, AND THEN WE CAN GET STARTED...

INTERVIEW!

WRITE!

EDIT!

RESEARCH!

ONE WEEK LATER...

LUIS?

DID MY MOM EMAIL YOU?

NO. WHY?

CHECK OUT THE COMMENTS ON THAT VIDEO YOU DID FOR YOUR PROJECT.

Comments

↑ ↓ Reply

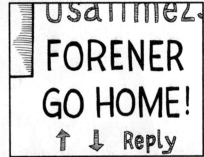

usanmez...
FORENER GO HOME!

↑ ↓ Reply

MOM WAS PRETTY UPSET.

SHE WANTED TO EMAIL YOU TO TAKE DOWN THE VIDEO, BUT SHE KNOWS IT'S IMPORTANT FOR YOUR PROJECT.

Disable Comments

CLICK

I CAN'T BELIEVE THE TERRIBLE THINGS PEOPLE WRITE IN ONLINE COMMENTS SOMETIMES.

IT'S LIKE THEY FORGET THEY'RE TALKING TO OTHER HUMAN BEINGS.

TELL ME ABOUT IT.

I'M REALLY SORRY THIS HAPPENED, BUT I'M GLAD YOU TOLD ME.

I'M DELETING THE COMMENT.

MAYBE I SHOULD EVEN MAKE THE VIDEO PRIVATE.

THAT'S NICE OF YOU...

BUT...

BUT WHAT?

I DUNNO... I'M SORRY MOM WAS UPSET, BUT IT SEEMS LIKE **CENSORSHIP** TO DELETE THE COMMENT.

REALLY!?!

I CAN'T BELIEVE YOU'D SAY THAT.

I KNOW, BUT THOSE VIEWS ARE OUT THERE... AND HIDING THEM WON'T MAKE THEM GO AWAY.

I THINK I'M GOING TO MENTION THIS INCIDENT IN MY INTRODUCTION, IF THAT'S OKAY WITH YOUR MOTHER.

LET ME EMAIL HER SO WE CAN TALK ABOUT IT.

ANOTHER WEEK LATER...

HEY, LUIS, CHECK THIS OUT.

MY MOM WENT TO THE MEDIA LAB AND MADE HER OWN VIDEO TO RESPOND TO THE COMMENT ABOUT HER INTERVIEW!

I KNOW THAT MY ADOPTED HOME, THE UNITED STATES, ENCOURAGES FREEDOM OF SPEECH...

...AND I'M DELIGHTED THAT BEING AN AMERICAN GIVES ME THE RIGHT TO TALK BACK TO THOSE WHO QUESTION MY CONTRIBUTIONS TO THIS COUNTRY...

WOW! GOOD FOR HER!

I KNOW. SHE ACTUALLY ROCKS SOMETIMES.

-HIGH-FIVE!

NOW YOU CAN POST THE ORIGINAL VIDEO WITH BOTH THE ANGRY COMMENT AND HER VIDEO RESPONSE...

...LIKE A **DIALOGUE** -- BUT ONE THAT MAKES A REALLY EFFECTIVE ARGUMENT!

ha ha ha

YOU KNOW MY MOM -- SHE ALWAYS GETS THE LAST WORD!

ha ha ha ha ha ha ha

DRAWING CONCLUSIONS

The following assignments ask you to think
about making your work available to audiences.

1 Choose an activity in which you're an expert -- a hobby, sport, craft, skill, or something else. Take notes about the activity: steps/processes, necessary materials, favorite memories, emotional responses, motivations for sticking with it, etc. Using your notes, draft a short poem about the activity. Then draft a short how-to tutorial about doing that same thing. Finally, compare the two texts and the experiences of writing in two different genres about the same topic.

Do the different genres speak to different audiences? Do they serve the same purposes? Do they use the same rhetorical strategies? Does your "voice," or the way you use your identity as an author, shift between the two genres? Why or why not?

2 Reflect on some of the research papers you've written in the past. What materials did you need, and what steps did you need to take to successfully complete them? Drawing from these experiences, write a "recipe for a successful research paper." List the necessary ingredients and quantities, and include detailed steps, in order, to ensure that a reader can follow your recipe. Look at some examples of recipes, and consider including a brief introductory blurb about the finished product, notes on appropriate pairings with this "dish," pro tips or warnings, or even step-by-step photos.

Does the recipe genre work for giving directions for completing a piece of writing? Why or why not? Did your recipe function as a serious set of directions or something else? How do the tone and purpose of your "recipe for a successful research paper" compare to those of a more conventional recipe?

3

Book trailers, short videos made by fans of books and published on YouTube, take the genre of the movie trailer and adapt it to generate excitement around a literary text. Part endorsement, part teaser, and part book report, book trailers serve as winks to fans or invitations to join a community of readers.

Spend some time checking out book trailers for books you may already love and books you may not be familiar with. Then, choose a book that you've recently read, and sketch out a storyboard for your own book trailer. What elements of the trailer must you include to make the genre recognizable to other viewers? What is the primary "message" and purpose of your trailer? For whom is your trailer designed? How have you communicated the essence of the book -- its genre, tone, and subject matter -- to your audience?

4

This chapter describes some ways that "going public" online can mean reaching unintended audiences, facing unforeseen consequences, or receiving unpleasant or unproductive feedback. Liz and Jonathan feel strongly that developing an awareness of both the advantages and the risks of publishing digital media is important for everyone.

Fables and fairy tales are short fictional forms that are intended to teach lessons to young people. After doing some research on these genres, draft a fable or fairy tale teaching the next generation (younger relatives or neighbors, for example) about using the Internet responsibly.

GLOSSARY

INDEX

GLOSSARY

Analysis
A close examination of the parts of a text with the goal of interpreting it as a whole.

Argument
The primary purpose of a text, or the main claim it makes.

Assertion
A debatable claim.

Audience
The intended or accidental recipients of a communication.

Cause and effect
Tracing the reasons that led to an outcome, or anticipating the likely result of an event or circumstance.

Citation
The way the original source of a quotation, summary, or paraphrase is documented.

Comparison and contrast
Noting similarities and differences between two texts.

Composition
Creating a text in one or more media.

Conclusion
The end of a text that ties together its argument.

Context
The situation in which a text is created, including its creator, audience, purpose, medium, and genre, as well as other factors.

Credibility
The characteristic that makes a text believable.

Critical lens
A perspective or theoretical approach that provides a context for analysis.

Critical reading
An analytical approach to a text.

Discourse
Written or spoken communication, often characterized by its use in particular communities.

Ethos
The credibility or authority that a speaker or writer brings to a subject.

Evidence
The information used to support an argument.

Explication
Revealing or uncovering ideas that are not directly stated in a text.

Genre
A conventional format for presenting information and ideas.

Implicit messages
Ideas that are present in a text but not directly stated.

Integration
Weaving material from others' work into one's own text and adding commentary that explains the material's purpose and importance.

Interpretation
Using context and critical analysis to explain the meaning of a text.

Invention
Any technique (such as freewriting or brainstorming) for exploring new thoughts and ideas during the writing process.

Kairos
Awareness of the appropriate timing, occasion, or opportunity for a given rhetorical act.

Logos
Appeals to reason and logic in a text.

Medium (*plural,* Media)
Material that records, displays, stores, or spreads information.

Paraphrase
A detailed explanation of the contents of a source that rephrases the language of the original source.

Pathos
Appeals to emotion.

Peer revision *or* Peer review
The process of seeking feedback on a text from a classmate, colleague, or friend.

Plagiarism
Presenting the work of another as one's own, whether accidentally or deliberately.

Primary source
A work that presents a firsthand account of an event or a time.

Purpose
The aim of a communication.

Quotation
Direct repetition of material from a source.

Reflection
In writing, an analysis of a completed project that considers what the writer learned during the writing process.

Remediation
Revising a text that appeared originally in one medium so that it is effective in another medium.

Revision
The process of rewriting to improve a text, often by viewing it from different perspectives.

Rhetoric
The practice or study of effective communication.

Rhetorical analysis
Examining how, what, and why a given text communicates.

Secondary source
A work that describes, analyzes, or interprets a firsthand account or original work.

Summary
A brief, general restatement of the content of a source.

Surface errors
Distracting mistakes in grammar, punctuation, or spelling.

Synthesis
Putting information from multiple sources together to make one unified meaning.

Text
In rhetorical terms, any communication in any medium—including print books, films, Web content, slide presentations, Facebook posts, and so on.

Thesis
The main idea that a text develops.

Tone
The attitude that a text conveys to an audience.

Visual literacy
The ability to analyze elements of a visual text.

Voice
In writing, the way a writer expresses the person behind the words.

Writing process
The steps writers take in composing a text, which can vary greatly from writer to writer and from situation to situation.

INDEX

Index

Index

community.macmillan.com

macmillanlearning.com

bedford/st.martin's
Macmillan Learning

ISBN 978-1-319-06260-6

9 781319 062606

T2-DKQ-125